Holt McDougal Mathematics

Grade 7
Know-It Notebook™

HOLT McDOUGAL

COMMON CORE EDITION

HOUGHTON MIFFLIN HARCOURT

Copyright © by Houghton Mifflin Harcourt Publishing Company

All rights reserved. No part of this work may be reproduced or transmitted in any
form or by any means, electronic or mechanical, including photocopying or recording,
or by any information storage or retrieval system, without the prior written permission
of the copyright owner unless such copying is expressly permitted by federal
copyright law.

Permission is hereby granted to individuals using the corresponding student's
textbook or kit as the major vehicle for regular classroom instruction to photocopy
entire pages from this publication in classroom quantities for instructional use and
not for resale. Requests for information on other matters regarding duplication of
this work should be addressed to Houghton Mifflin Harcourt Publishing Company,
Attn: Contracts, Copyrights, and Licensing, 9400 South Park Center Loop, Orlando,
Florida 32819.

Printed in the U.S.A.

ISBN 978-0-547-68785-8

2 3 4 5 6 7 8 9 10   1689   20 19 18 17 16 15 14 13 12 11

4500317609   ^ B C D E F G

If you have received these materials as examination copies free of charge,
Houghton Mifflin Harcourt Publishing Company retains title to the materials and
they may not be resold. Resale of examination copies is strictly prohibited.

Possession of this publication in print format does not entitle users to convert this
publication, or any portion of it, into electronic format.

Contents

© Houghton Mifflin Harcourt Publishing Company

Holt McDougal Mathematics

Contents

© Houghton Mifflin Harcourt Publishing Company

Holt McDougal Mathematics

Introduction

Using the Know-It Notebook™

This *Know-It Notebook* will help you take notes, organize your thinking, and study for quizzes and tests. There are *Know-It Notes*™ pages for every lesson in your textbook. These notes will help you identify important mathematical information that you will need later.

Know-It Notes
Lesson Objectives
A good note-taking practice is to know the objective the content covers.

Vocabulary
Another good note-taking practice is to keep a list of the new vocabulary.
- Use the page references or the glossary in your textbook to find each definition.
- Write each definition on the lines provided.

Additional Examples
Your textbook includes examples for each math concept taught. Additional examples in the *Know-It Notebook* help you take notes so you remember how to solve different types of problems.
- Take notes as your teacher discusses each example.
- Write notes in the blank boxes to help you remember key concepts.
- Write final answers in the shaded boxes.

Check It Out!
Complete the Check It Out! problems that follow some lessons. Use these to make sure you understand the math concepts covered in the lesson.
- Write each answer in the space provided.
- Check your answers with your teacher or another student.
- Ask your teacher to help you understand any problem that you answered incorrectly.

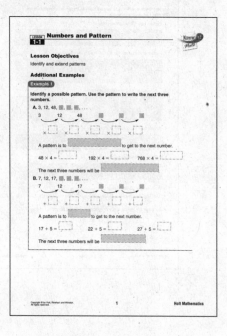

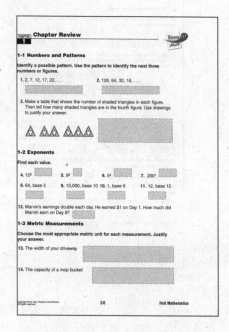

© Houghton Mifflin Harcourt Publishing Company

Holt McDougal Mathematics

Introduction

Chapter Review

Complete Chapter Review problems that follow each chapter. This is a good review before you take the chapter test.

- Write each answer in the space provided.
- Check your answers with your teacher or another student.
- Ask your teacher to help you understand any problem that you answered incorrectly.

Big Ideas

The Big Ideas have you summarize the important chapter concepts in your own words. You must think about and understand ideas to put them in your own words. This will also help you remember them.

- Write each answer in the space provided.
- Check your answers with your teacher or another student.
- Ask your teacher to help you understand any question that you answered incorrectly.

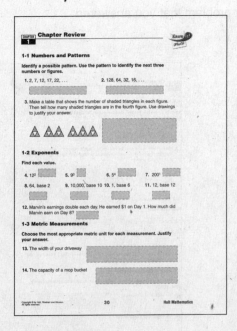

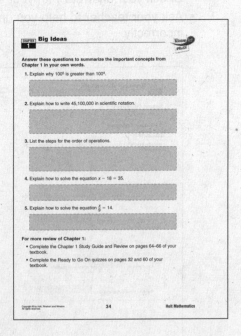

© Houghton Mifflin Harcourt Publishing Company

Holt McDougal Mathematics

Introduction

Note Taking Strategies

Taking good notes is very important in many of your classes and will be even more important when you take college classes. This notebook was designed to help you get started. Here are some other steps that can help you take good notes.

Getting Ready

1. Use a loose-leaf notebook. You can add pages to this where and when you want to. It will help keep you organized.

During the Lecture

2. If you are taking notes during a lecture, write the big ideas. Use abbreviations to save time. Do not worry about spelling or writing every word. Use headings to show changes in the topics discussed. Use numbering or bullets to organize supporting ideas under each topic heading. Leave space before each new heading so that you can fill in more information later.

After the Lecture

3. As soon as possible after the lecture, read through your notes and add any information that will help you understand them when you review later. You should also summarize the information into key words or key phrases. This will help your comprehension and will help you process the information. These key words and key phrases will be your memory cues when you are reviewing for or taking a test. At this time you may also want to write questions to help clarify the meaning of the ideas and facts.

4. Read your notes out loud. As you do this, state the ideas in your own words and do as much as you can by memory. This will help you remember and will also help with your thinking process. This activity will help you understand the information.

5. Reflect upon the information you have learned. Ask yourself how new information relates to information you already know. Ask how this relates to your personal experience. Ask how you can apply this information and why it is important.

Before the Test

6. Review your notes. Don't wait until the night before the test to review. Do frequent reviews. Don't just read through your notes. Put the information in your notes into your own words. If you do this you will be able to connect the new material with material you already know, and you will be better prepared for tests. You will have less test anxiety and better recall.

7. Summarize your notes. This should be in your own words and should only include the main points you need to remember. This will help you internalize the information.

© Houghton Mifflin Harcourt Publishing Company

Holt McDougal Mathematics

Algebraic Reasoning
Order of Operations

Lesson Objectives

Use the order of operations to simplify numerical expressions

Vocabulary

numerical expression _____

_____

order of operations _____

_____

_____

Additional Examples

Example 1

Simplify each expression.

A. $3 + 15 \div 5$

   $3 + 15 \div 5$ Divide.

   $3 + \boxed{}$ Add.

B. $44 - 14 \div 2 \cdot 4 + 6$

   $44 - 14 \div 2 \cdot 4 + 6$ $\boxed{}$ and $\boxed{}$ from left
   to right.

   $44 - \boxed{} \cdot 4 + 6$

   $44 - \boxed{} + 6$ $\boxed{}$ and $\boxed{}$ from left to right.

   $\boxed{} + 6$

© Houghton Mifflin Harcourt Publishing Company

Algebraic Reasoning

Order of Operations, continued

Example 2

Simplify each expression.

A. $42 - (3 \cdot 4) \div 6$

$42 - (3 \cdot 4) \div 6$ Perform the operation inside the

$42 - \boxed{} \div 6$

$42 - \boxed{}$

B. $[(26 - 4 \cdot 5) + 6]^2$

$[(26 - 4 \cdot 5) + 6]^2$ The parentheses are inside the brackets, so

perform the operations inside the

$\boxed{}$ first.

$[(26 - \boxed{}) + 6]^2$

$[\boxed{} + \boxed{}]^2$

$\boxed{}^2$

Example 3

Sandy runs 4 miles per day. She ran 5 days during the first week of the month. She ran only 3 days each week for the next 3 weeks. Simplify the expression $(5 + 3 \cdot 3) \cdot 4$ to find how many miles she ran last month.

$(5 + 3 \cdot 3) \cdot 4$ Perform the operations inside the

$\boxed{}$ first.

$(5 + \boxed{}) \cdot 4$ Add.

$\boxed{} \cdot 4$ Multiply.

$\boxed{}$

Sandy ran $\boxed{}$ miles last month.

© Houghton Mifflin Harcourt Publishing Company

Algebraic Reasoning
Order of Operations, continued

Check It Out!

1. Simplify the expression.

   $2 + 24 \div 6$

2. Simplify the expression.

   $24 - (4 \cdot 5) \div 4$

3. **Jill is learning vocabulary words for a test. From the list, she already knew 30 words. She is learning 4 new words a day for 3 days each week. Evaluate the expression $3 \cdot 4 \cdot 7 + 30$ to find out how many words she will know at the end of seven weeks.**

© Houghton Mifflin Harcourt Publishing Company

Holt McDougal Mathematics

LESSON 2	**Algebraic Reasoning**
	Properties of Numbers

Lesson Objectives

Identify properties of numbers and use them to simplify numerical expressions

Vocabulary

Commutative Property _____

_____

Associative Property _____

_____

Identity Property _____

_____

Distributive Property _____

_____

Additional Examples

Example 1

Tell which property is represented.

A. $(2 \cdot 6) \cdot 1 = 2 \cdot (6 \cdot 1)$

$(2 \cdot 6) \cdot 1 = 2 \cdot (6 \cdot 1)$ The numbers are [_____].

B. $3 + 0 = 3$

$3 + 0 = 3$ The sum of 3 and [__] is 3.

C. $7 + 9 = 9 + 7$

$7 + 9 = 9 + 7$ The order of the numbers is [_____].

© Houghton Mifflin Harcourt Publishing Company

Algebraic Reasoning

Properties of Numbers, continued

Example 2

Simplify each expression. Justify each step.

A. 21 + 16 + 9

$21 + 16 + 9 =$ ☐ $+$ ☐ $+ 9$ _____ Property

$= 16 + (21 + 9)$ _____ Property

$= 16 +$ ☐   Add.

$=$ ▨

B. 20 · 9 · 5

$20 · 9 · 5 = 20 ·$ ☐ $·$ ☐ _____ Property

$= (20 · 5) · 9$ _____ Property

$=$ ☐ $· 9$ Multiply.

$=$ ▨

Example 3

Use the Distributive Property to find 6(54).

Method 1: $6(54) = 6($ ☐ $+$ ☐ $)$ Rewrite 54 as ☐ $+$ ☐ .

$= (6 ·$ ☐ $) + (6 ·$ ☐ $)$ Use the _____ Property.

$=$ ☐ $+$ ☐   Multiply.

$=$ ▨   Add.

© Houghton Mifflin Harcourt Publishing Company

LESSON 2 — Algebraic Reasoning

Properties of Numbers, continued

Use the Distributive Property to find 6(54).

Method 2: $6(54) = 6(\boxed{} - \boxed{})$ Rewrite 54 as $\boxed{} - \boxed{}$.

$= (6 \cdot \boxed{}) - (6 \cdot \boxed{})$ Use the $\boxed{}$ Property.

$= \boxed{} - \boxed{}$ Multiply.

$= \boxed{}$ Subtract.

Check It Out!

1. Tell which property is represented.

$(5 + 6) + 3 = 5 + (6 + 3)$

2. Simplify the expression. Justify each step.

$215 + 73 + 85$

3. Use the Distributive Property to find 7(18).

6

Holt McDougal Mathematics

© Houghton Mifflin Harcourt Publishing Company

Algebraic Reasoning
Variables and Algebraic Expressions

Lesson Objectives

Evaluate algebraic expressions

Vocabulary

variable _____

_____

constant _____

_____

algebraic expression _____

_____

evaluate _____

_____

Additional Examples

Example 1

Evaluate *k* + 9 for each value of *k*.

A. *k* = 5   *k*   + 9

 + 9   Substitute ☐ for *k*.

[ ]   Add.

B. *k* = 2   *k*   + 9

 + 9   Substitute ☐ for *k*.

[ ]   Add.

Holt McDougal Mathematics

© Houghton Mifflin Harcourt Publishing Company

Algebraic Reasoning

Variables and Algebraic Expressions, continued

Example 2

Evaluate each expression for the given value of the variable.

A. $4x - 3$ for $x = 2$

$4(\boxed{}) - 3$ Substitute $\boxed{}$ for x.

               Multiply.

$\boxed{} - 3$ Subtract.

B. $s \div 5 + s$, for $s = 15$

$\boxed{} \div 5 + \boxed{}$ Substitute 15 for $\boxed{}$.

               Divide.

$\boxed{} + 15$ Add.

Example 3

Evaluate $\dfrac{6}{a} + 4b$, for $a = 3$ and $b = 2$.

$\dfrac{6}{a} + 4b$

$\boxed{} + 4(\boxed{})$ Substitute $\boxed{}$ for a and $\boxed{}$ for b.

               Divide and multiply from $\boxed{}$ to $\boxed{}$.

$\boxed{} + \boxed{}$ Add.

Check It Out!

1. Evaluate $a + 6$ for the value of a.

     $a = 3$

© Houghton Mifflin Harcourt Publishing Company

Algebraic Reasoning

LESSON 4

Translating Words into Math

Lesson Objectives

Translate words into numbers, variables, and operations

Additional Examples

Example 1

Write each phrase as an algebraic expression.

A. the quotient of a number and 4

quotient means "[   ]"

[   ]

B. *w* increased by 5

increased by means "[   ]"

[   ]

C. the difference of 3 times a number and 7

[   ] · [   ] − 7

[   ]

D. the quotient of 4 and a number, increased by 10

[   ]

© Houghton Mifflin Harcourt Publishing Company

Algebraic Reasoning

Translating Words into Math, continued

LESSON 4

Example 2

A. Mr. Campbell drives at 55 mi/h. Write an expression for how far he can drive in *h* hours.

You need to put _____ parts together. This involves multiplication.

55mi/h · *h* hours = _____

B. On a history test Maritza scored 50 points on the essay. Besides the essay, each short-answer question was worth 2 points. Write an expression for her total points if she answered *q* short-answer questions correctly.

The total points include ____ points for each short-answer question.

Multiply to put _____ parts together: _____

In addition to the points for short-answer questions, the total points

included ____ points on the essay.

Add to put the parts together: _____

Check It Out!

1. Write the phrase as an algebraic expression.

4 times the difference of *y* and 8

2. Julie Ann works on an assembly line building computers. She can assemble 8 units an hour. Write an expression for the number of units she can produce in *h* hours.

© Houghton Mifflin Harcourt Publishing Company

Holt McDougal Mathematics

Algebraic Reasoning

Simplifying Algebraic Expressions

Know it! Note

Lesson Objectives

Simplify algebraic expressions

Vocabulary

term _____

_____

coefficient _____

_____

Additional Examples

Example 1

Identify like terms in the list.

| $3t$ | $5w^2$ | $7t$ | $9v$ | $4w^2$ | $8v$ |

Look for like [ ] with like [ ].

$3t$ $5w^2$ $7t$ $9v$ $4w^2$ $8v$

Like terms: [ ]

Example 2

Simplify. Justify your steps using the Commutative, Associative, and Distributive Properties when necessary.

A. $6t - 4t$ $6t$ and $4t$ are [ ] terms.

$6t - 4t$ [ ] the coefficients.

[ ]

B. $45x - 37y + 87$

In this expression, there are [ ] to combine.

© Houghton Mifflin Harcourt Publishing Company

Holt McDougal Mathematics

Algebraic Reasoning

Simplifying Algebraic Expressions, continued

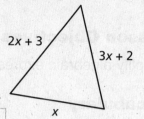

Example 3

Write an expression for the perimeter of the triangle. Then simplify the expression.

$x + 3x + 2 + 2x + 3$ Write an [_____] using the side lengths.

$(\boxed{} + \boxed{} + \boxed{}) + (\boxed{} + \boxed{})$ Identify and [____] like terms.

$\boxed{}$ $\boxed{}$ like terms.

Check It Out!

1. Identify like terms in the list.

$2x \qquad 4y^3 \qquad 8x \qquad 5z \qquad 5y^3 \qquad 8z$

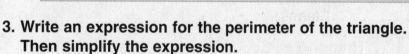

2. Simplify. Justify your steps using the Commutative, Associative, and Distributive Properties when necessary.

$4x^2 + 4y + 3x^2 - 4y + 2x^2 + 5$

3. Write an expression for the perimeter of the triangle. Then simplify the expression.

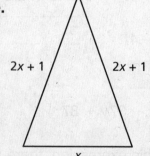

Holt McDougal Mathematics

© Houghton Mifflin Harcourt Publishing Company

Algebraic Reasoning
Chapter Review

Know it! Note

1 Order of Operations

Simplify each expression.

1. $2 + 7 \cdot 9 - 4$

2. $[(2 + 4)^2 \div 12]^3$

3. $4^2 \div (1 + 7)^2 \cdot 12$

Compare. Write $<$, $>$, or $=$.

4. $14 - 2 \cdot 2$ ▮ $7 + 6 \div 3$

5. $18 \div 2 + 3$ ▮ $5 \cdot 4 - 8$

6. $7 + (8 - 4)^2$ ▮ $6^2 - 11$

7. $19 + 7^2 \div 2$ ▮ $(4 + 4)^2$

2 Properties of Numbers

Tell which property is represented.

8. $2 \cdot (4 \cdot 3) = (2 \cdot 4) \cdot 3$

9. $7 + 5 = 5 + 7$

10. $5 \cdot 1 = 5$

Use the Distributive Property to find each product.

11. $5(11 + 7) =$

12. $(19 + 3)2 =$

© Houghton Mifflin Harcourt Publishing Company

Holt McDougal Mathematics

Algebraic Reasoning
Chapter Review, continued

3 Variables and Algebraic Expressions

Evaluate $n + 8$ for each value of n.

13. $n = 4$

14. $n = 0$

15. $n = 10$

16. $n = 17$

Evaluate each expression for the given value of the variable.

17. $10x + 9$ for $x = 3$

18. $14y - 6$ for $y = 5$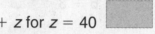

19. $2c^2 + 4c$ for $c = 4$

20. $z \div 8 + z$ for $z = 40$

Evaluate each expression for the given values of the variables.

21. $\dfrac{15}{y} + 6z$ for $y = 3$ and $z = 7$

22. $12p - 4q + 9$ for $p = 2$ and $q = 1$

4 Translating Words Into Math

Write each phrase as an algebraic expression.

23. 12 less than a number

24. the sum of 6 and a number

25. 5 times a number

26. 4 divided into a number

27. The Cookie Factory sold q chocolate chip cookies for $0.45 each. Write an algebraic expression for the amount sold.

5 Simplifying Algebraic Expressions

Identify like terms in each list.

28. x y^2 x^4 $2y^2$ $\dfrac{x}{5}$ $4y$

29. 4 p^3 $7q$ $2q^2$ $9p^3$ 13

Simplify each expression.

30. $2e + 4f + 7e$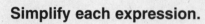

31. $b^2 + 2c + 9b^2 + 2$

© Houghton Mifflin Harcourt Publishing Company

Holt McDougal Mathematics

Algebraic Reasoning

LESSON 1

Big Ideas

Answer these questions to summarize the important concepts from Chapter 1 in your own words.

1. List the steps for the order of operations.

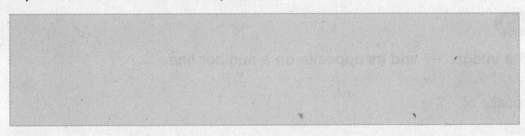

2. Explain how to evaluate the expression $x - 18$ for $x = 29$.

For more review of Chapter 1:

• Complete the Chapter 1 Study Guide and Review in your textbook.

• Complete the Ready to Go On quizzes in your textbook.

© Houghton Mifflin Harcourt Publishing Company

Integers and Rational Numbers

Integers

Lesson Objectives

Compare and order integers and determine absolute value

Vocabulary

opposite _____

additive inverse _____

integers _____

absolute value _____

_____

Additional Examples

Example 1

Graph the integer −7 and its opposite on a number line.

The opposite of −7 is [ ] .

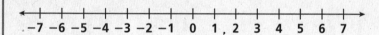

Example 2

Compare the integers. Use < or >.

A. 4 [ ] −4

4 is farther to the [   ] than −4, so 4 [ ] −4.

B. −15 [ ] −9

−15 is farther to the [   ] than −9, so −15 [ ] −9.

Holt McDougal Mathematics

© Houghton Mifflin Harcourt Publishing Company

Integers and Rational Numbers
Integers, continued

Example 3

Use a number line to order the integers from least to greatest.

−3, 6, −5, 2, 0, −8

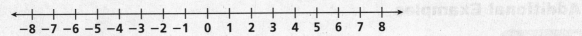

Example 4

Use a number line to find each absolute value.

A. $|8|$

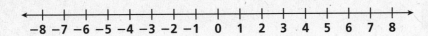

8 is 8 units from 0, so $|8|$ = ▢.

B. $|−12|$

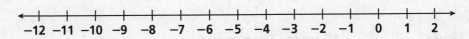

−12 is 12 units from 0, so $|−12|$ = ▢.

Check It Out!

1. Graph the integer 5 and its opposite on a number line.

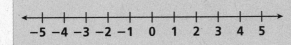

2. Compare the integers. Use < or >.

−7 ▢ −10

© Houghton Mifflin Harcourt Publishing Company

Integers and Rational Numbers

Adding Integers

Lesson Objectives

Add integers

Additional Examples

Example 1

Use a number line to find each sum.

A. $-7 + (-4)$

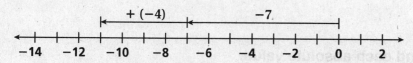

Start at 0. Move left ☐ units. Then move left ☐ more units.

$-7 + (-4) = $ ☐

B. $-12 + 19$

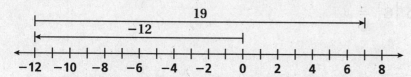

Start at ☐. Move ☐ 12 units. Then move ☐ 19 units.

$-12 + 19 = $ ☐

Example 2

Find each sum.

A. $-4 + 8$ The signs are ☐.

Find the difference of the ☐ values.
Think: $8 - 4 = 4$.

☐   Use the sign of the integer with the ☐ absolute value (positive).

© Houghton Mifflin Harcourt Publishing Company

Integers and Rational Numbers

Find each sum.

B. $23 + (-35)$ The [ ] are different.

$23 + (-35)$ Find the [ ] of the absolute values.

[ ] Think: [ ] $-$ [ ] $= 12$.

Use the [ ] of the integer with the greater absolute

value ([ ]).

Example 3

Evaluate $x + y$ for $x = -42$ and $y = 71$.

$x + y$ Substitute [ ] for x and [ ] for y.

[ ] $+$ [ ] The signs are [ ].

Find the [ ] of the absolute values.

Think: [ ] $-$ [ ] $= 29$.

[ ] Use the sign of the integer with the greater absolute

[ ] (positive).

© Houghton Mifflin Harcourt Publishing Company

Example 4

The jazz band's income from a bake sale was $286. Expenses were $21.
Use integer addition to find the band's total profit or loss.

$286 + (-21)$ Use negative for the [＿＿＿＿].

$286 - 21$ Find the [＿＿＿＿] of the absolute
values.

[＿＿＿].   The [＿＿＿] is positive.

The band's profit was $[＿＿＿].

Check It Out!

1. Use a number line to find the sum.

$-4 + (-5)$

2. Find the sum.

$-13 + (-24)$

3. Evaluate $x + y$ for $x = -24$ and $y = 17$.

**4. The French Club was raising money for a trip to Washington D. C.
Their carwash raised $730. They had expenses of $52. Use integer
addition to find the club's total profit or loss.**

© Houghton Mifflin Harcourt Publishing Company

LESSON 3 **Integers and Rational Numbers**
Subtracting Integers

Lesson Objectives

Subtract integers

Additional Examples

Example 1

Use a number line to find each difference.

A. $4 - 1$

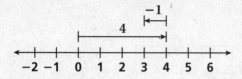

Start at 0. Move right ⬜ units. To subtract ⬜, move to the left.

$4 - 1 =$ ⬜

B. $-3 - 1$

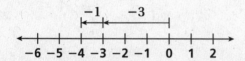

⬜ at 0. Move 3 units ⬜. To subtract 1, move to

the ⬜. $-3 - 1 =$ ⬜

Example 2

Find each difference.

A. $5 - (-2)$

$5 + 2$ Add the ⬜ of -2.

⬜

B. $-3 - 7$

⬜ $+$ ⬜   Add the opposite of 7.

⬜

© Houghton Mifflin Harcourt Publishing Company

Holt McDougal Mathematics

Example 3

Evaluate *x* − *y* for each set of values.

A. $x = -3$ and $y = 2$

$x - y$

$-3 - 2 = \boxed{} + (\boxed{})$ $\boxed{}$ for *x* and *y*.

$= \boxed{}$ Add the opposite of $\boxed{}$.

B. $x = 4$ and $y = -6$

$x - y$

$4 - (-6) = \boxed{} + \boxed{}$ Substitute for $\boxed{}$ and $\boxed{}$.

$= \boxed{}$ Add the $\boxed{}$ of −6.

Example 4

Find the difference between 32 °F and −10 °F.

$\boxed{} - (\boxed{})$

$32 \boxed{} 10 = \boxed{}$ Add the opposite of $\boxed{}$.

The difference in temperature is $\boxed{}$ °F.

© Houghton Mifflin Harcourt Publishing Company

Integers and Rational Numbers

Subtracting Integers, continued

Check It Out!

1. Use a number line to find the difference.

    $-4 - (-2)$

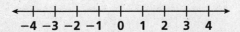

2. Find the difference.

    $-1 - 4$

3. Evaluate $x - y$ for the set of values.

    $x = -4$ and $y = -3$

4. Find the difference between 8 °F and −5 °F.

© Houghton Mifflin Harcourt Publishing Company

Integers and Rational Numbers
Multiplying and Dividing Integers

Lesson Objectives

Multiply and divide integers

Additional Examples

Example 1

Use a number line to find each product.

A. $-7 \cdot 2$

$-7 \cdot 2 = 2 \cdot (-7)$

= [　　　　]

<---+---+---+---+---+---+---+---+--->
  -14 -12 -10 -8 -6 -4 -2   0   2

Use the Commutative Property.

Think: Add -7 [　　　] times.

B. $-8 \cdot 3$

$-8 \cdot 3 = 3 \cdot (-8)$

= [　　　　]

<---+---+---+---+---+---+---+---+--->
 -24 -20 -16 -12 -8 -4   0   4

Use the Commutative Property.

Think: Add -8 [　　　] times.

Example 2

Find each product.

A. $-6 \cdot (-5)$

$-6 \cdot (-5) = $ [　　　]   Both signs are [　　　　　], so the product

is [　　　　　].

B. $-4 \cdot 7$

$-4 \cdot 7 = $ [　　　]   The signs are [　　　　　], so the

product is [　　　　　].

© Houghton Mifflin Harcourt Publishing Company

Example 3

Find each quotient.

A. $35 \div (-5)$

$35 \div (-5)$ Think: $35 \div \boxed{} = 7$.

   The $\boxed{}$ are different, so the $\boxed{}$

is negative.

B. $-32 \div (-8)$

$-32 \div (-8)$ Think: $32 \div 8 = 4$.

   The signs are $\boxed{}$, so the quotient is

$\boxed{}$.

C. $-48 \div 6$

$-48 \div 6$ Think: $48 \div 6 = \boxed{}$.

The signs are $\boxed{}$, so the quotient is

$\boxed{}$.

Example 4

Mrs. Johnson kept track of a stock she was considering buying. She recorded the price change each day. What was the average change per day?

Mon	Tues	Wed	Thu	Fri
–$1	$3	$2	–$5	$6

Find the $\boxed{}$ of the changes in price.

$\dfrac{5}{5} = \boxed{}$ Divide to find the average.

The average change was $\$\boxed{}$ per day.

© Houghton Mifflin Harcourt Publishing Company
Holt McDougal Mathematics

Integers and Rational Numbers

Multiplying and Dividing Integers, continued

Check It Out!

1. Use a number line to find the product.

$-5 \cdot 3$

2. Find the product.

$-2 \cdot (-8)$

3. Find the quotient.

$-12 \div 3$

4. Mr. Reid kept track of his blood sugar daily. He recorded the change each day. What was the average change per day?

Day	Mon	Tues	Wed	Thu	Fri
Unit Change	−8	2	4	−9	−6

© Houghton Mifflin Harcourt Publishing Company

Holt McDougal Mathematics

LESSON 5 Integers and Rational Numbers
Solving Equations Containing Integers

Lesson Objectives

Solve one-step equations with integers

Additional Examples

Example 1

Solve each equation. Check your answer.

A. $-6 + x = -7$

$$+\boxed{} \quad +\boxed{}$$

$\boxed{}$ Add $\boxed{}$ to both sides to isolate the variable.

$x = \boxed{}$

B. $p + 5 = -3$

$$+\,(\boxed{}) \quad +\,(\boxed{})$$

Add $\boxed{}$ to both sides to $\boxed{}$ the variable.

$p = \boxed{}$

C. $y - 9 = -40$

$$+\boxed{} \quad +\boxed{}$$

Add $\boxed{}$ to both sides to $\boxed{}$ the variable.

$y = \boxed{}$

Example 2

Solve each equation. Check your answer.

A. $\dfrac{b}{-5} = 6$

$$\dfrac{b}{-5} = 6$$

$$(\boxed{})\dfrac{b}{-5} = (\boxed{})6 \qquad \text{Multiply both sides by } \boxed{}.$$

$b = \boxed{}$

© Houghton Mifflin Harcourt Publishing Company

B. $-400 = 8y$

$$-400 = 8y$$

$$\frac{-400}{\boxed{}} = \frac{8y}{\boxed{}}$$ Divide both sides by $\boxed{}$.

$$\boxed{} = y$$

Example 3

In 2007, a manufacturer made a profit of $300 million. This amount was $100 million more than the profit in 2006. What was the profit in 2006?

Let p represent the profit in 2006 (in millions of dollars).

Profit in 2007 $= p + \boxed{}$

Profit in 2007 $= \$\boxed{}$ million

$p + \quad 100 = \quad 300$

$\underline{-\boxed{}} \quad \underline{-\boxed{}}$

$p = \boxed{}$

The profit in 2006 was $\$\boxed{}$ million.

Check It Out!

1. Solve the equation. Check the answer.

$y - 7 = -34$

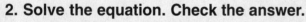

2. Solve the equation. Check the answer.

$\frac{c}{4} = -24$

© Houghton Mifflin Harcourt Publishing Company

Integers and Rational Numbers

Equivalent Fractions and Decimals

Lesson Objectives

Write fractions as decimals, and vice versa, and determine whether a decimal is terminating or repeating

Vocabulary

terminating decimal _____

repeating decimal _____

Additional Examples

Example 1

Write each fraction as a decimal. Round to the nearest hundredth, if necessary.

A. $\frac{1}{4}$

B. $\frac{9}{5}$

C. $\frac{5}{3}$

```
       [   ]                    [   ]                    [   ]
    4)1.00                   5)9.0                     3)5.00
     −8                       −5                        −3
     ───                      ───                       ───
      20                       4 0                       2 0
     −20                      −4 0                       −1 8
     ───                      ───                       ───
       0                        0                         2 0
                                                         −1 8
                                                         ───
                                                           2
```

$\frac{1}{4} =$ [   ] $\frac{9}{5} =$ [   ] $\frac{5}{3} \approx$ [   ]

Example 2

Write each fraction as a decimal.

A. $\frac{4}{5}$

$\frac{4}{5} \times \dfrac{[\ \ ]}{[\ \ ]} = \dfrac{[\ \ ]}{[\ \ ]}$ Multiply to get a power of [   ] in the denominator.

= , [   ]

Holt McDougal Mathematics

© Houghton Mifflin Harcourt Publishing Company

Integers and Rational Numbers

Equivalent Fractions and Decimals, continued

B. $\dfrac{37}{50}$

$$\dfrac{37}{50} \times \dfrac{\boxed{}}{\boxed{}} = \dfrac{\boxed{}}{\boxed{}}$$

Multiply to get a power of $\boxed{}$ in the denominator.

$$= \boxed{}$$

Example 3

Write each decimal as a fraction in simplest form.

A. 0.018

$$0.018 = \dfrac{18}{1,000} = \dfrac{18 \div 2}{1,000 \div 2} = \boxed{}$$

B. 1.55

$$1.55 = \dfrac{155}{100} = \dfrac{155 \div 5}{100 \div 5} = \boxed{} \text{ or } \boxed{}$$

Example 4

A football player completed 1,546 of the 3,875 passes he attempted. Find his completion rate. Write your answer as a decimal rounded to the nearest thousandth.

Fraction	What the Calculator Shows	Completion Rate
	1546 ÷ 3875 ENTER 0.398967749	

His completion rate is $\boxed{}$.

Check It Out!

1. Write the fraction as a decimal. Round to the nearest hundredth, if necessary.

$$\dfrac{6}{5}$$

 © Houghton Mifflin Harcourt Publishing Company **Holt McDougal Mathematics**

Integers and Rational Numbers

Comparing and Ordering Rational Numbers

Lesson Objectives

Compare and order fractions and decimals

Vocabulary

rational number _____

_____

Additional Examples

Example 1

Compare the fractions. Write < or >.

A. $\dfrac{7}{9}$ ▨ $\dfrac{5}{8}$

Both fractions can be written with a [   ] of 72.

$\dfrac{7}{9} = \dfrac{7 \cdot \boxed{}}{9 \cdot \boxed{}} = \boxed{}$ Write as fractions with [   ] denominators.

$\dfrac{5}{8} = \dfrac{5 \cdot \boxed{}}{8 \cdot \boxed{}} = \boxed{}$

$\boxed{} > \boxed{}$, and so $\dfrac{7}{9}$ ▨ $\dfrac{5}{8}$.   Compare the numerators.

B. $-\dfrac{2}{5}$ ▨ $-\dfrac{3}{7}$

Both fractions can be written with a [   ] of 35.

$-\dfrac{2}{5} = \dfrac{-2 \cdot \boxed{}}{5 \cdot \boxed{}} = \boxed{}$ Write as fractions with common [   ].

$-\dfrac{3}{7} = \dfrac{-3 \cdot \boxed{}}{7 \cdot \boxed{}} = \boxed{}$ Put the negative signs in the numerators.

$-\boxed{} > -\boxed{}$, and so $-\dfrac{2}{5}$ ▨ $-\dfrac{3}{7}$.

© Houghton Mifflin Harcourt Publishing Company

Holt McDougal Mathematics

Example 2

Compare the decimals. Write < or >.

A. 0.427  0.425

0.427   Line up the [_____] points.

The tenths and hundredths are the [_____].

0.425   Compare the [_____] : 7 [____] 5.

0.427 ⇅

0.427 [____] 0.425

B. 0.7$\overline{3}$ [____] 0.734   [_____] is a repeating decimal.

0.7$\overline{3}$ = 0.733   Line up the [_____] points.

The tenths and hundredths are the [_____].

0.734   Compare the [_____] : 3 [____] 4.

0.7$\overline{3}$ [____] 0.734

© Houghton Mifflin Harcourt Publishing Company

Example 3

Order $\frac{4}{5}$, 0.93, and 0.9 from least to greatest.

Write as decimals with the same number of places.

$\frac{4}{5}$ = 0.80   0.93 = [ ]   0.9 = [ ]

Graph the numbers on a number line.

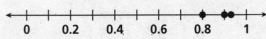

The values on a number line [   ] as we move from left to right.

0.80 < 0.90 < 0.93   Place the decimals in [   ].

[   ]

Check It Out!

1. Compare the fractions. Write < or >.

$\frac{5}{6}$ ■ $\frac{7}{8}$

$\frac{5}{6}$ [   ] $\frac{7}{8}$

2. Compare the decimals. Write < or >.

0.535 ■ 0.538

0.535 [   ] 0.538

3. Order $\frac{3}{5}$, 0.84, and 0.7 from least to greatest.

[   ]

© Houghton Mifflin Harcourt Publishing Company

Integers and Rational Numbers
Chapter Review

1 Integers

Compare the integers. Use < or >.

1. 4 −6

2. −2 2

3. −14 −9

Use a number line to find each absolute value.

4. $|-6|$

5. $|3|$

6. $|-9|$

2 Adding Integers

Find each sum.

7. $-8 + 6$

8. $13 + (-3)$

9. $-7 + (-4)$

Evaluate $a + b$ for the given values.

10. $a = 8, b = -17$

11. $a = -44, b = 49$

12. $a = -5, b = -14$

3 Subtracting Integers

Find each difference.

13. $7 - 11$

14. $-9 - (-15)$

15. $-7 - 6$

Evaluate $a - b$ for the given values.

16. $a = 8, b = -3$

17. $a = -4, b = 11$

18. $a = 3, b = 8$

© Houghton Mifflin Harcourt Publishing Company

Holt McDougal Mathematics

4 Multiplying and Dividing Integers

Find each product.

19. $6 \cdot (-3)$

20. $-4 \cdot 8$

21. $-8 \cdot (-5)$

Find each quotient.

22. $45 \div (-9)$

23. $-24 \div 4$

24. $-39 \div (-3)$

5 Solving Equations Containing Integers

Solve. Check your answer.

25. $8h = -48$

26. $-15 + k = 35$

27. $27 - x = -42$

28. This year, 84 students performed at the Spring Choral Concert. There were 4 groups with an equal number of students that performed. How many students were in each group?

6 Equivalent Fractions and Decimals

Write each fraction as a decimal.

29. $\frac{2}{5}$

30. $\frac{7}{20}$

31. $\frac{37}{50}$

32. $\frac{5}{8}$

Write each decimal as a fraction in simplest form.

33. 0.075

34. -1.15

35. 0.38

36. -2.8

© Houghton Mifflin Harcourt Publishing Company

7 Comparing and Ordering Rational Numbers

Compare the fractions. Write < or >.

37. $\dfrac{3}{5}$ ▨ $\dfrac{2}{3}$

38. $-\dfrac{6}{5}$ ▨ $-\dfrac{5}{6}$

39. $-\dfrac{4}{7}$ ▨ $-\dfrac{5}{9}$

Compare the decimals. Write < or >.

40. 0.378 ▨ 0.375

41. -0.19 ▨ -0.919

42. -5.9 ▨ 5.09

Holt McDougal Mathematics

© Houghton Mifflin Harcourt Publishing Company

Integers and Rational Numbers
Big Ideas

Answer these question to summarize the important concepts from Chapter 2 in your own words.

1. Explain why −5 and 5 have the same absolute value.

2. Explain how to find the sign of the answer when subtracting integers.

3. Explain how to find the sign of the answer when multiplying or dividing integers.

For more review of Chapter 2:

• Complete the Chapter 2 Study Guide and Review in your textbook.

• Complete the Ready to Go On quizzes in your textbook.

© Houghton Mifflin Harcourt Publishing Company

Holt McDougal Mathematics

Applying Rational Numbers

Adding and Subtracting Decimals

Lesson Objectives

Add and subtract decimals

Additional Examples

Example 1

Add. Estimate to check whether each answer is reasonable.

A. $4.55 + 11.3$

4.55	Line up the [____] points.
$+ 11.30$	Use [____] as a placeholder.
[____]	Add.

Estimate

$5 + 11 =$ [____]   [____] is a reasonable answer.

B. $-8.33 + (-10.972)$

$-8.33 + (-10.972)$	Think: [____] + [____]
8.330	Line up the [____] points.
$+ 10.972$	Use zero as a [____].
[____]	Add.

$-8.33 + (-10.972) =$ [____]

Estimate

[____] + [____] $= -19$ -19.302 is a [____] answer.

Holt McDougal Mathematics

© Houghton Mifflin Harcourt Publishing Company

Applying Rational Numbers

Adding and Subtracting Decimals, continued

Example 2

Subtract.

A. $5.34 - 2.08$

$$
\begin{array}{r}
5.34 \\
-\ 2.08 \\
\hline
\end{array}
$$

☐☐☐☐☐ up the decimal points.

Subtract.

B. $28 - 15.911$

$$
\begin{array}{r}
\overset{7\ \ 9\ 9\ 10}{28.000} \\
-\ 15.911 \\
\hline
\end{array}
$$

Use zeros as placeholders.
Line up the decimal points.

Subtract.

Example 3

During one month in the United States, 492.23 million commuter trips were taken on buses, and 26.331 million commuter trips were taken on light rail. What was the total number of trips taken on buses and light rail? Estimate to check whether your answer is reasonable.

$$
\begin{array}{r}
492.230 \\
+\ 26.331 \\
\hline
\end{array}
$$

Line up the decimal ☐☐☐☐☐ .

Use ☐☐☐☐☐ as a placeholder.

Add.

Estimate

☐☐☐ + ☐☐☐ = 518   ☐☐☐☐ is a reasonable answer.

The total number of trips was ☐☐☐☐☐ million.

Check It Out!

1. Add. Estimate to check whether the answer is reasonable.

$-7.89 + (-13.852)$ ☐☐☐☐☐☐

© Houghton Mifflin Harcourt Publishing Company

Holt McDougal Mathematics

Applying Rational Numbers

Multiplying Decimals

Lesson Objectives

Multiply decimals

Additional Examples

Example 1

Multiply.

A. 7 · 0.1

    7   0 decimal places
 × 0.1   1 decimal place

           0 + 1 = 1 decimal place.

B. −3 · 0.03

   −3   0 decimal places
 × 0.03   2 decimal places

           0 + 2 = 2 decimal places. Use [   ] as a placeholder.

C. 2.45 · 35

  2.45   [ ] decimal places

 × 35   [ ] decimal places

           [ ] + [ ] = [ ] decimal places.

Example 2

Multiply. Estimate to check whether each answer is reasonable.

A. 2.4 · 1.8

   2.4   1 decimal place
 × 1.8   1 decimal place
  1 92
+ 2 40

           1 + 1 = 2 decimal places.

Estimate

  2 · 2 = 4   [   ] is a reasonable answer.

Holt McDougal Mathematics

© Houghton Mifflin Harcourt Publishing Company

Applying Rational Numbers
Multiplying Decimals, continued

Multiply. Estimate to check whether each answer is reasonable.

B. $-3.84 \cdot 0.9$

$$
\begin{array}{rl}
-3.84 & \text{2 decimal places} \\
\times\, 0.9 & \text{1 decimal place} \\
\hline
\boxed{} & \\
& 2 + 1 = 3 \text{ decimal places.}
\end{array}
$$

Estimate

$-4 \cdot 1 = -4$ $\boxed{}$ is a $\boxed{}$ answer.

Example 3

To find your weight on another planet, multiply the relative gravitational pull of the planet and your weight. The relative gravitational pull on Mars is 0.38. What would a person who weighs 85 pounds on Earth weigh on Mars?

$$
\begin{array}{rl}
85 & \boxed{}\ \text{decimal places} \\
\times\, 0.38 & \boxed{}\ \text{decimal places} \\
\hline
680 & \\
+\, 2550 & \boxed{} + \boxed{} = \boxed{}\ \text{decimal places} \\
\hline
\boxed{} &
\end{array}
$$

The person would weigh $\boxed{}$ pounds on Mars.

Estimate

$85 \times 0.5 = \boxed{}$ $\boxed{}$ is a reasonable answer.

Check It Out!

1. Multiply.

$3.65 \cdot 15$ $\boxed{}$

2. Multiply. Estimate to check whether the answer is reasonable.

$3.2 \cdot 1.6$ $\boxed{}$

© Houghton Mifflin Harcourt Publishing Company

Holt McDougal Mathematics

Applying Rational Numbers

Dividing Decimals

Lesson Objectives

Divide decimals

Additional Examples

Example 1

Divide.

A. 8.28 ÷ 4.6

8.28 ÷ 4.6 = 82.8 ÷ 46   Multiply both numbers by ⬚ to make the
                                 divisor an integer.

$$\begin{array}{r} 46\overline{)82.8} \\ \underline{46} \\ 36\ 8 \\ \underline{-36\ 8} \\ 0 \end{array}$$ Divide as with whole numbers.

B. 18.48 ÷ (−1.75)

18.48 ÷ (−1.75) = 1,848 ÷ 175   Multiply both numbers by ⬚
                                        to make the divisor an integer.

$$\begin{array}{r} 175\overline{)1848.00} \\ \underline{-175} \\ 98\ 0 \\ \underline{-87\ 5} \\ 10\ 50 \\ \underline{-10\ 50} \\ 0 \end{array}$$ Use ⬚ as placeholders.
                                        Divide as with whole numbers.

18.48 ÷ (−1.75) = ⬚   The signs are ⬚.

© Houghton Mifflin Harcourt Publishing Company

Applying Rational Numbers

Dividing Decimals, continued

Example 2

Divide. Estimate to check whether each answer is reasonable.

A. 4 ÷ 1.25

4.00 ÷ 1.25 = 400 ÷ 125   [   ] both numbers by 100.

```
      3.2
125)400.0
   -375
     25 0
    -25 0
        0
```

Use zero as a [   ].
Divide as with whole numbers.

Estimate

4 ÷ 1 = 4   The answer is [   ].

B. −24 ÷ (−2.5)

−24.0 ÷ (−2.5) = −240 ÷ (−25)   Multiply both numbers by [   ].

```
      9.6
25)240.0
  -225
    15 0
   -15 0
        0
```

Divide as with whole numbers.

Estimate

−24 ÷ (−3) = 8   The answer is [   ].

© Houghton Mifflin Harcourt Publishing Company

Applying Rational Numbers

Dividing Decimals, continued

Example 3

Eric paid $229.25 to rent a car. The fee to rent the car was $32.75 per day. For how long did Eric rent the car?

229.25 ÷ 32.75 = 22,925 ÷ 3,275   Multiply both numbers by ▢ .

3,275)22,925   Divide as with whole numbers.
– 22,925
        0

Eric rented the car for ▢ days.

Check It Out!

1. Divide.

6.45 ÷ 0.5

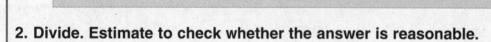

2. Divide. Estimate to check whether the answer is reasonable.

−22 ÷ (−2.5)

3. Jace took a trip in which he drove 350 miles. During the trip his truck used 12.5 gallons of gas. What was his truck's gas mileage?

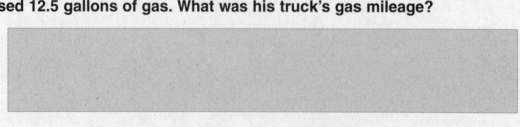

© Houghton Mifflin Harcourt Publishing Company

LESSON 4 — Applying Rational Numbers

Solving Equations Containing Decimals

Lesson Objectives

Solve one-step equations that contain decimals

Additional Examples

Example 1

Solve. Justify your steps.

A. $n - 2.75 = 8.3$

$n - 2.75 \quad = \quad 8.30$ Use the [   ] Property of Equality.

$+ [\quad] \qquad + [\qquad]$ Add [\qquad] to both sides.

$n \quad = \quad$ [   ]

B. $a + 32.66 = 42$

$a + 32.66 \quad = \quad 42.00$ Use the [   ] Property of Equality.

$- [\qquad] \qquad - [\qquad]$ Subtract [\qquad] from both sides.

$a \quad = \quad$ [   ]

Example 2

Solve. Justify your steps.

A. $\dfrac{x}{4.8} = 5.4$

$\dfrac{x}{4.8} = 5.4$ Use the [   ] Property of Equality.

$\dfrac{x}{4.8} \cdot [\quad] = 5.4 \cdot [\quad]$ Multiply both sides by [\quad].

$x = $ [   ]

© Houghton Mifflin Harcourt Publishing Company

Applying Rational Numbers

Solving Equations Containing Decimals, continued

Solve.

B. $9 = 3.6d$

$9 = 3.6d$ Use the ☐ Property of Equality.

$\dfrac{9}{\boxed{}} = \dfrac{3.6d}{\boxed{}}$ Divide both sides by ☐.

☐ $= d$ Think: $9 \div 3.6 = 90 \div 36$

☐ $= d$

Example 3   **PROBLEM SOLVING APPLICATION**

A board-game box is 2.5 inches tall. A toy store has shelving space measuring 15 inches vertically in which to store the boxes. How many boxes can be stacked in the space?

1. Understand the Problem

Rewrite the question as a statement.

Find the number of boxes that can be placed on the shelf.
List the important information:

A. Each board-game box is ☐ inches tall.

B. The store has shelving space measuring ☐ inches.

2. Make a Plan

The total height of the boxes is equal to the height of one box ☐ the number of boxes. Since you know how tall the shelf is you can write an equation with *b* being the number of boxes.

☐ $b = 15$

© Houghton Mifflin Harcourt Publishing Company

Holt McDougal Mathematics

Applying Rational Numbers

Solving Equations Containing Decimals, continued

3. Solve

$$2.5b = 15$$

$$\frac{2.5b}{\boxed{}} = \frac{2.5}{\boxed{}}$$ Divide to $\boxed{}$ b.

$$b = \boxed{}$$

$\boxed{}$ boxes can be stacked in the space.

4. Look Back

You can round 2.5 to $\boxed{}$ and estimate how many boxes will fit on the shelf.

$$15 \div \boxed{} = 5$$

So $\boxed{}$ boxes is a reasonable answer.

Check It Out!

1. Solve.

$$a + 27.51 = 36$$

2. Solve.

$$9 = 2.5d$$

3. A canned good is 4.5 inches tall. A grocery store has shelving space measuring 18 inches vertically in which to store the cans. How many cans can be stacked in the space?

© Houghton Mifflin Harcourt Publishing Company

Holt McDougal Mathematics

Applying Rational Numbers

Adding and Subtracting Fractions

Lesson Objectives

Add and subtract fractions

Additional Examples

Example 1

Add or subtract. Write each answer in simplest form.

A. $\frac{5}{8} + \frac{1}{8}$

$\frac{5}{8} + \frac{1}{8} = \frac{\boxed{} + \boxed{}}{8}$ Add the $\boxed{}$ and keep the $\boxed{}$.

$= \boxed{} = \boxed{}$ Simplify.

B. $\frac{9}{11} - \frac{4}{11}$

$\frac{9}{11} - \frac{4}{11} = \frac{\boxed{} - \boxed{}}{11}$ Subtract the $\boxed{}$ and keep

the $\boxed{}$.

$= \boxed{}$ The answer is in the simplest form.

Example 2

Add or subtract. Write each answer in simplest form.

A. $\frac{5}{6} + \frac{7}{8}$

$\frac{5}{6} + \frac{7}{8} = \frac{5 \cdot 4}{6 \cdot 4} + \frac{7 \cdot 3}{8 \cdot 3}$ The LCM of the denominator is $\boxed{}$.

$= \boxed{} + \boxed{}$ Write equivalent $\boxed{}$ using

the common $\boxed{}$.

$= \boxed{} = \boxed{}$ Add.

© Houghton Mifflin Harcourt Publishing Company

Applying Rational Numbers

Adding and Subtracting Fractions, continued

Add or subtract. Write each answer in simplest form.

B. $\dfrac{2}{3} - \dfrac{3}{4}$

$$\dfrac{2}{3} - \dfrac{3}{4} = \dfrac{2 \cdot 4}{3 \cdot 4} - \dfrac{3 \cdot 3}{4 \cdot 3}$$

Multiply the [   ].

$$= \boxed{} - \boxed{}$$

Write [   ] fractions

using the [   ] denominator.

$$= \boxed{}$$

Subtract.

Example 3

In one Earth year, Jupiter completes about $\dfrac{1}{12}$ of its orbit around the Sun, while Mars completes about $\dfrac{1}{2}$ of its orbit. How much more of its orbit does Mars complete than Jupiter?

$$\dfrac{1}{2} - \dfrac{1}{12} = \boxed{} - \dfrac{1}{12}$$

The LCM of the denominators is [   ].

$$= \boxed{} - \dfrac{1}{12}$$

Write [   ] fractions

using the common [   ].

$$= \boxed{}$$

Subtract.

Mars completes [   ] more of its orbit than Jupiter does.

Check It Out!

1. Add. Write the answer in simplest form.

$$\dfrac{5}{6} + \dfrac{1}{6}$$

2. Subtract. Write the answer in simplest form.

$$\dfrac{2}{5} - \dfrac{1}{2}$$

© Houghton Mifflin Harcourt Publishing Company

Holt McDougal Mathematics

Applying Rational Numbers

Multiplying Fractions and Mixed Numbers

Lesson Objectives

Multiply fractions and mixed numbers

Additional Examples

Example 1

Multiply. Write each answer in simplest form.

A. $-12 \cdot \frac{3}{4}$

$$-12 \cdot \frac{3}{4} = \boxed{} \cdot \frac{3}{4} \qquad \text{Write } -12 \text{ as a} \boxed{}.$$

$$= -\frac{\overset{3}{\cancel{12}} \cdot 3}{1 \cdot \underset{1}{\cancel{4}}} \qquad \text{Simplify.}$$

$$= \boxed{} = \boxed{} \qquad \boxed{} \text{ numerators.}$$

$$\boxed{} \text{ denominators.}$$

B. $\frac{1}{3} \cdot \frac{3}{8}$

Simplify.

$$\frac{1}{3} \cdot \frac{3}{8} = \frac{1 \cdot \overset{1}{\cancel{3}}}{\underset{1}{\cancel{3}} \cdot 8} \qquad \boxed{} \text{ numerators.}$$

$$\boxed{} \text{ denominators.}$$

$$= \boxed{}$$

Example 2

Multiply. Write each answer in simplest form.

A. $\frac{2}{5} \cdot 1\frac{2}{3}$

$$\frac{2}{5} \cdot 1\frac{2}{3} = \frac{2}{5} \cdot \boxed{} \qquad \text{Write the} \boxed{} \text{ number as an}$$

$$\text{improper} \boxed{}.$$

$$= \frac{2}{\underset{1}{\cancel{5}}} \cdot \frac{\overset{1}{\cancel{5}}}{3} \qquad \text{Simplify.}$$

$$= \boxed{} \qquad \boxed{} \text{ numerators.}$$

$$\boxed{} \text{ denominators.}$$

Holt McDougal Mathematics

© Houghton Mifflin Harcourt Publishing Company

Applying Rational Numbers

Multiplying Fractions and Mixed Numbers, continued

Multiply. Write each answer in simplest form.

B. $4\frac{1}{5} \cdot 2\frac{1}{7}$

$4\frac{1}{5} \cdot 2\frac{1}{7} = \boxed{} \cdot \boxed{}$ Write the mixed $\boxed{}$ as

$\boxed{}$ fractions.

$= \dfrac{{}^{3}\cancel{21} \cdot \cancel{15}^{3}}{{}_{1}\cancel{5} \cdot \cancel{7}_{1}}$ Simplify.

$= \boxed{}$ or $\boxed{}$ Multiply $\boxed{}$.

Multiply $\boxed{}$.

Example 3

In 2001, the car toll on the George Washington Bridge was \$6.00. In 1995, the toll was $\frac{2}{3}$ of that toll. What was the toll in 1995?

$6 \cdot \boxed{} = \boxed{} + \boxed{} + \boxed{} + \boxed{} + \boxed{} + \boxed{}$

$= \boxed{}$

$= \boxed{}$ Simplify.

$= \$\boxed{}$ Write the fraction as a decimal.

The George Washington Bridge toll for a car was \$ $\boxed{}$ in 1995.

Check It Out!

1. In 2002, the fee to park in a parking garage was \$4. In 2000, the fee was $\frac{3}{4}$ of the fee in 2002. What was the fee in 2000?

2. Multiply. Write the answer in simplest form.

$-\dfrac{3}{7} \cdot \dfrac{1}{8}$

© Houghton Mifflin Harcourt Publishing Company

Applying Rational Numbers
Dividing Fractions and Mixed Numbers

Lesson Objectives

Divide fractions and mixed numbers

Vocabulary

reciprocal _____

multiplicative inverse _____

Additional Examples

Example 1

Divide. Write each answer in simplest form.

A. $\frac{3}{7} \div \frac{2}{5}$

$\frac{3}{7} \div \frac{2}{5} = \frac{3}{7} \cdot \boxed{}$ Multiply by the $\boxed{}$ of $\frac{2}{5}$.

$= \frac{3 \cdot 5}{7 \cdot 2}$

$= \boxed{}$ or $\boxed{}$

B. $\frac{3}{8} \div 12$

$\frac{3}{8} \div 12 = \frac{3}{8} \cdot \boxed{}$

$= \frac{\overset{1}{\cancel{3}}}{8} \cdot \frac{1}{\underset{4}{\cancel{12}}}$ Multiply by the $\boxed{}$ of 12.

$= \boxed{}$ Simplify.

Holt McDougal Mathematics

© Houghton Mifflin Harcourt Publishing Company

Applying Rational Numbers

Dividing Fractions and Mixed Numbers, continued

Example 2

Divide. Write each answer in simplest form.

A. $5\frac{2}{3} \div 1\frac{1}{4}$

$5\frac{2}{3} \div 1\frac{1}{4} = \boxed{} \div \boxed{}$ Write mixed $\boxed{}$ as

improper $\boxed{}$.

$= \frac{17}{3} \cdot \boxed{}$ Multiply by the $\boxed{}$

of $\frac{5}{4}$.

$= \boxed{}$ or ▮

B. $\frac{3}{4} \div 2\frac{1}{2}$

$\frac{3}{4} \div 2\frac{1}{2} = \frac{3}{4} \div \boxed{}$ Write $2\frac{1}{2}$ as an $\boxed{}$ fraction.

$= \frac{3}{4} \cdot \boxed{}$

$= \dfrac{3 \cdot \overset{1}{\cancel{2}}}{\underset{2}{\cancel{4}} \cdot 5}$ Multiply by the $\boxed{}$ of $\frac{5}{2}$.

$= $ ▮   Simplify.

C. $5\frac{5}{8} \div \frac{5}{9}$

$5\frac{5}{8} \div \frac{5}{9} = \boxed{} \div \frac{5}{9}$ Write $5\frac{5}{8}$ as an $\boxed{}$ fraction.

$= \frac{45}{8} \cdot \boxed{}$ Multiply by the $\boxed{}$

of $\frac{5}{9}$.

$= \dfrac{45 \cdot \overset{9}{9}}{8 \cdot \underset{1}{\cancel{5}}}$

$= \boxed{}$ or ▮

© Houghton Mifflin Harcourt Publishing Company

Holt McDougal Mathematics

Applying Rational Numbers

Dividing Fractions and Mixed Numbers, continued

Example 3

The life span of a golden dollar coin is 30 years, while paper currency lasts an average of $1\frac{1}{2}$ years. How many times longer will the golden dollar stay in circulation?

$$30 \div 1\frac{1}{2} = \frac{30}{1} \div \frac{3}{2}$$ Write the number as an [＿＿＿＿] fraction.

$$= \frac{30}{1} \cdot \boxed{}$$ Multiply by the [＿＿＿＿＿＿] of $\frac{3}{2}$.

$$= \frac{^{10}30 \cdot 2}{1 \cdot 3_1}$$ Simplify.

$$= \boxed{} \text{ or } \boxed{}$$

The golden dollar will stay in circulation about [＿＿＿] times longer than paper currency.

Check It Out!

1. Divide. Write the answer in simplest form.

$$\frac{3}{5} \div \frac{1}{2}$$

2. Divide. Write the answer in simplest form.

$$\frac{3}{5} \div 1\frac{2}{5}$$

3. The average life of a queen ant is approximately 3 years. The life span of a worker ant is $\frac{3}{7}$ year. How many times longer will the queen ant live?

© Houghton Mifflin Harcourt Publishing Company

Applying Rational Numbers

Solving Equations Containing Fractions

Lesson Objectives

Solve one-step equations that contain fractions

Additional Examples

Example 1

Solve. Write each answer in simplest form.

A. $x - \frac{3}{7} = \frac{5}{7}$

$$x - \frac{3}{7} = \frac{5}{7}$$

$$x - \frac{3}{7} + \boxed{} = \frac{5}{7} + \boxed{} \qquad \text{Use the } \boxed{} \text{ Property of Equality.}$$

$$x = \boxed{} = \boxed{} \qquad \text{Add.}$$

B. $\frac{4}{9} + r = -\frac{1}{2}$

$$\frac{4}{9} + r = -\frac{1}{2}$$

$$\frac{4}{9} + r - \boxed{} = -\frac{1}{2} - \boxed{} \qquad \text{Use the } \boxed{} \text{ Property of}$$

Equality.

$$r = \boxed{} - \boxed{} \qquad \text{Find a common } \boxed{}.$$

$$r = \boxed{} \qquad \text{Subtract.}$$

Example 2

Solve. Write each answer in simplest terms.

A. $\frac{3}{8}x = \frac{1}{4}$

$$\frac{3}{8}x = \frac{1}{4}$$

$$\frac{3}{8}x \cdot \frac{8}{3} = \frac{1}{\overset{}{\underset{1}{4}}} \cdot \frac{\overset{2}{8}}{3} \qquad \text{Multiply by the } \boxed{} \text{ of } \frac{3}{8}.$$

$$x = \boxed{} \qquad \text{Then simplify.}$$

© Houghton Mifflin Harcourt Publishing Company

Holt McDougal Mathematics

Applying Rational Numbers

Solving Equations Containing Fractions, continued

B. $4y = \dfrac{8}{9}$

$4y = \dfrac{8}{9}$ Use the Multiplicative Inverse Property.

$4y \cdot \dfrac{1}{4} = \dfrac{\overset{2}{8}}{9} \cdot \dfrac{1}{\underset{1}{4}}$ Multiply by the reciprocal of $\boxed{}$.

$y = \boxed{}$ Then simplify.

Example 3

The amount of copper in brass is $\dfrac{3}{4}$ of the total weight. If a sample contains $4\dfrac{1}{5}$ ounces of copper, what is the total weight of the sample?

Let w represent the total weight of the sample.

$\dfrac{3}{4}w = 4\dfrac{1}{5}$ Write an equation.

$\dfrac{3}{4}w \cdot \boxed{} = 4\dfrac{1}{5} \cdot \boxed{}$ Multiply by the $\boxed{}$ of $\dfrac{3}{4}$.

$w = \dfrac{\overset{7}{21}}{} \cdot \dfrac{4}{\underset{1}{\cancel{3}}}$ Write $4\dfrac{1}{5}$ as an $\boxed{}$ fraction.

$w = \boxed{}$ or $\boxed{}$ Then simplify.

The sample weighs ounces.

Check It Out!

1. Solve. Write the answer in simplest form.

$x - \dfrac{3}{8} = \dfrac{7}{8}$

© Houghton Mifflin Harcourt Publishing Company

Holt McDougal Mathematics

Applying Rational Numbers

Chapter Review

Know it! Note

1 Adding and Subtracting Decimals

Add or subtract. Estimate to check whether each answer is reasonable.

1. $-3.817 + 4.2$ **2.** $7.624 - 18.34$ **3.** $-4.77 - 12.053$ **4.** $30.62 - (-9.18)$

5. The table shows the top 5 movies of all time and the amount each made in profit.

Movie	$ (million)
Titanic (1997)	600.8
Star Wars (1977)	460.9
Shrek 2 (2004)	436.5
E. T. The Extra-Terrestrial (1982)	434.9
Star Wars Episode I –The Phantom Menace (1999)	431.1

  a) How much more money did Titanic (1997) make in profit than Star Wars (1977)?

  b) How much money have the top 3 movies made in profit altogether?

2 Multiplying Decimals

Multiply. Estimate to check whether each answer is reasonable.

6. $-8.7 \cdot 3.12$ **7.** $1.89 \cdot 0.07$ **8.** $-5.21 \cdot (-43.6)$ **9.** $0.58 \cdot (-3.1)$

10. Fresh ground beef is on sale for $4.90 per pound. How much will it cost to buy 8.30 pounds of ground beef?

© Houghton Mifflin Harcourt Publishing Company

Applying Rational Numbers

Chapter Review, continued

3 Dividing Decimals

Divide. Estimate to check whether each answer is reasonable

11. $48 \div 3.2$ **12.** $-13.6 \div 1.6$ **13.** $72 \div (-3.2)$ **14.** $-154 \div (-0.35)$

4 Solving Equations Containing Decimals

Solve.

15. $t - 0.94 = 18.5$ **16.** $w + 28.52 = -16.03$

17. $0.27x = -8.1$ **18.** $\dfrac{k}{-0.36} = 8.5$

19. Shea bought CDs for $11.65 each. She spent a total of $163.10. How many CDs did Shea buy?

5 Adding and Subtracting Fractions

Find each sum or difference. Write your answer in simplest form.

20. $-\dfrac{1}{4} + \dfrac{3}{8} + \dfrac{5}{12}$ **21.** $\dfrac{5}{6} - \dfrac{3}{15} - \dfrac{2}{5}$

22. Kevin ran for $\dfrac{3}{4}$ hour, swam for $\dfrac{1}{2}$ hour, and bicycled for $\dfrac{5}{6}$ hour. How long did Kevin run, swim, and bike altogether?

6 Multiplying Fractions and Mixed Numbers

Complete each multiplication sentence.

23. $\dfrac{2}{3} \cdot \dfrac{\blacksquare}{9} = \dfrac{10}{27}$ **24.** $\dfrac{7}{8} \cdot \dfrac{2}{\blacksquare} = \dfrac{7}{12}$ **25.** $\dfrac{9}{\blacksquare} \cdot \dfrac{4}{5} = \dfrac{9}{25}$

26. Caitlin drove at 65 mph for $6\dfrac{3}{4}$ hours. How many miles did she travel?

© Houghton Mifflin Harcourt Publishing Company

Holt McDougal Mathematics

7 Dividing Fractions and Mixed Numbers

Evaluate. Write each answer in simplest form.

27. $\frac{5}{6} \cdot \frac{2}{3} \div 2\frac{2}{9}$

28. $3\frac{1}{3} \div (\frac{3}{5} \cdot \frac{1}{2})$

29. Tommy and his three brothers worked for $177\frac{3}{5}$ hours. What was the average number of hours each brother worked?

8 Solving Equations Containing Fractions

Solve. Write each answer in simplest form.

30. $-\frac{17}{55} + d = \frac{28}{55}$

31. $2\frac{5}{18}p = 5\frac{4}{9}$

32. Mark spends $\frac{1}{3}$ of his day sleeping and $\frac{1}{4}$ of his day at school. What fraction is spent doing things besides sleeping and going to school?

© Houghton Mifflin Harcourt Publishing Company

Holt McDougal Mathematics

Applying Rational Numbers

Big Ideas

Answer these questions to summarize the important concepts from Chapter 3 in your own words.

1. Explain how to multiply decimals.

2. Explain how to divide an integer by a decimal.

3. Explain the difference between adding or subtracting fractions with unlike denominators, and multiplying fractions with unlike denominators.

For more review of Chapter 3:

- Complete the Chapter 3 Study Guide and Review in your textbook.
- Complete the Ready to Go On quizzes in your textbook.

© Houghton Mifflin Harcourt Publishing Company

Holt McDougal Mathematics

Proportional Relationships
Rates

Lesson Objectives

Find and compare unit rates, such as average speed and unit price

Vocabulary

rate _____

_____

unit rate _____

_____

Additional Examples

Example 1

Find each rate.

A. A Ferris wheel revolves 35 times in 105 minutes. How many minutes does 1 revolution take?

$\dfrac{\boxed{} \text{ minutes}}{\boxed{} \text{ revolutions}}$

Write a rate that compares minutes and revolutions.

$\dfrac{\boxed{} \text{ minutes} \div \boxed{}}{\boxed{} \text{ revolutions} \div \boxed{}}$

Divide the numerator and denominator by $\boxed{}$.

$\dfrac{\boxed{} \text{ minutes}}{1 \text{ revolution}}$

Simplify.

The Ferris wheel takes $\boxed{}$ minutes for 1 revolution.

© Houghton Mifflin Harcourt Publishing Company

Holt McDougal Mathematics

Proportional Relationships
Rates, continued

B. Sue walks 6 yards and passes 24 security lights set along the sidewalk. How many security lights does she pass in 1 yard?

$$\frac{\boxed{} \text{ lights}}{\boxed{} \text{ yards}}$$

Write a rate that compares lights and yards.

$$\frac{\boxed{} \text{ lights} \div \boxed{}}{\boxed{} \text{ yards} \div \boxed{}}$$

Divide the numerator and denominator by $\boxed{}$.

$$\frac{\boxed{} \text{ lights}}{1 \text{ yard}}$$

Simplify.

Sue walks past $\boxed{}$ security lights in 1 yard.

Example 2

Danielle is cycling 68 miles as a fundraising commitment. She wants to complete her ride in 4 hours. What should be her average speed in miles per hour?

$$\frac{\boxed{} \text{ miles}}{\boxed{} \text{ hours}}$$

Write the rate as a fraction.

$$\frac{\boxed{} \text{ miles} \div \boxed{}}{\boxed{} \text{ hours} \div \boxed{}} = \frac{\boxed{} \text{ miles}}{1 \text{ hour}}$$

Divide the numerator and denominator by $\boxed{}$.

Her average speed should be $\boxed{}$ miles per hour.

© Houghton Mifflin Harcourt Publishing Company

Proportional Relationships

Rates, continued

Example 3

A 12-ounce sports drink costs $0.99, and a 16-ounce drink costs $1.19. Which size is the better buy?

Divide the [ ] by the number of [ ] (oz) to find the unit price of each size.

$$\frac{\$ \boxed{}}{\boxed{} \text{ oz}} \approx \frac{\$ \boxed{}}{\boxed{} \text{ oz}} \qquad \frac{\$ \boxed{}}{\boxed{} \text{ oz}} \approx \frac{\$ \boxed{}}{\boxed{} \text{ oz}}$$

Since $ [ ] < $ [ ], the [ ]-oz sports drink is the better buy.

Check It Out!

1. Find the rate.

A car gets 189 miles with 9 gallons of gas. How many miles does the car get in 1 gallon of gas?

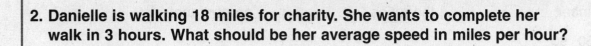

2. Danielle is walking 18 miles for charity. She wants to complete her walk in 3 hours. What should be her average speed in miles per hour?

3. A 28-ounce box of cereal costs $2.99, and a 32-ounce box of cereal costs $3.19. Which size is the better buy?

© Houghton Mifflin Harcourt Publishing Company

Proportional Relationships

Identifying and Writing Proportions

Know it!
Note

Lesson Objectives

Find equivalent ratios and identify proportions

Vocabulary

equivalent ratios _____

_____

proportion _____

_____

Additional Examples

Example 1

Determine whether the ratios are proportional.

A. $\frac{24}{51}, \frac{72}{128}$

$\frac{24 \div 3}{51 \div 3} = \boxed{}$ Simplify $\frac{24}{51}$.

$\frac{72 \div 8}{128 \div 8} = \boxed{}$ Simplify $\frac{72}{128}$.

Since $\boxed{} \neq \boxed{}$, the ratios $\boxed{}$ proportional.

B. $\frac{150}{105}, \frac{90}{63}$

$\dfrac{150 \div \boxed{}}{105 \div \boxed{}} = \frac{10}{7}$ Simplify $\frac{150}{105}$.

$\frac{90 \div 9}{63 \div 9} = \boxed{}$ Simplify $\frac{90}{63}$.

Since $\frac{10}{7} \boxed{} \boxed{}$, the ratios $\boxed{}$ proportional.

© Houghton Mifflin Harcourt Publishing Company

Proportional Relationships

Identifying and Writing Proportions, continued

Example 2

Directions for making 12 servings of rice call for 3 cups of rice and 6 cups of water. For 40 servings, the directions call for 10 cups of rice and 19 cups of water. Determine whether the ratios of rice to water are proportional for both servings of rice.

Write the [ ] of rice to water for 12 servings and for 40 servings.

Ratio of rice to water, 12 servings: [ ]   Write the ratio as a fraction.

Ratio of rice to water, 40 servings: [ ]   Write the ratio as a fraction.

$\dfrac{3}{6} = \dfrac{3 \cdot 19}{6 \cdot 19} = $ [ ]   Write the ratios with a [ ]

denominator, such as 114.

$\dfrac{10}{19} = \dfrac{10 \cdot 6}{19 \cdot 6} = $ [ ]

Since [ ] $\neq$ [ ], the two ratios [ ] proportional.

Example 3

Find an equivalent ratio. Then write the proportion.

A. $\dfrac{3}{5}$

$\dfrac{3}{5} = \dfrac{3 \cdot 2}{5 \cdot 2} = $ [ ]   Multiply both the [ ] and

[ ] by any number such as 2.

 = [ ]   Write a [ ].

B. $\dfrac{28}{16}$

$\dfrac{28}{16} = \dfrac{28 \div 4}{16 \div 4} = $ [ ]   Divide both the [ ] and

[ ] by any number such as 4.

[ ] = [ ]   Write a [ ].

© Houghton Mifflin Harcourt Publishing Company

Proportional Relationships

Check It Out!

1. Determine whether the ratios are proportional.

   $\frac{54}{63}$, $\frac{72}{144}$

2. Use the data in the table to determine whether the ratios of beans to water are proportional for both servings of beans.

Servings of Beans	Cups of Beans	Cups of Water
8	4	3
35	13	9

3. Find a ratio equivalent to the ratio. Then use the ratios to find a proportion.

   $\frac{16}{12}$

© Houghton Mifflin Harcourt Publishing Company

Holt McDougal Mathematics

Proportional Relationships
Solving Proportions

Lesson Objectives

Solve proportions by using cross products

Vocabulary

cross product _____

_____

Additional Examples

Example 1

Use cross products to solve the proportion.

$$\frac{9}{15} = \frac{m}{5}$$

◻ · m = ◻ · 5   The cross products are ◻.

◻ m = ◻   Multiply.

◻ = ◻   Divide each side by ◻ to isolate the variable.

m = ◻

Example 2 PROBLEM SOLVING APPLICATION

If 3 binders of the same size take up 4 inches of space on a shelf, how much space will be needed for 26 binders?

1. **Understand the Problem**

   Rewrite the question as a statement.

   • Find the space needed for ◻ binders.

   List the important information:

   • ◻ binders take up ◻ inches of space.

2. **Make a Plan**

   Set up a proportion using the given information.

   $$\frac{3 \text{ binders}}{4 \text{ inches}} = \frac{26 \text{ binders}}{x}$$ Let x be the unknown space.

© Houghton Mifflin Harcourt Publishing Company

Holt McDougal Mathematics

Proportional Relationships

Solving Proportions, *continued*

3. Solve

$\dfrac{3}{4} = \dfrac{26}{x}$

Write the [   ].

[   ] · x = 4 · [   ]

The cross products are [   ].

[   ] x = 104

Multiply.

[   ] = [   ]

Divide each side by [   ] to isolate the variable.

x = [   ]

[   ]

inches are needed for all 26 binders.

4. Look Back

$\dfrac{3}{4} = \dfrac{26}{34\frac{2}{3}}$

$4 \cdot 26 = 104$

$3 \cdot 34\frac{2}{3} = 104$

The cross products are equal, so $34\frac{2}{3}$ is the answer.

Check It Out!

1. Use cross products to solve the proportion.

$\dfrac{6}{7} = \dfrac{m}{14}$

[   ]

2. John filled his new radiator with 6 pints of coolant, which is to the 10 inch mark. How many pints of coolant would be needed to fill the radiator to the 25 inch level?

[   ]

© Houghton Mifflin Harcourt Publishing Company

Holt McDougal Mathematics

Proportional Relationships

Similar Figures and Proportions

Lesson Objectives

Use ratios to determine if two figures are similar

Vocabulary

similar _____

_____

corresponding sides _____

_____

corresponding angles _____

_____

Additional Examples

Example 1

Tell whether the triangles are similar.

$\overline{AB}$ corresponds to [ ].

$\overline{BC}$ corresponds to [ ].

$\overline{AC}$ corresponds to [ ].

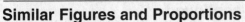

$\dfrac{AB}{DE} \overset{?}{=} \dfrac{BC}{EF} \overset{?}{=} \dfrac{AC}{DF}$

Write [ ] using the corresponding sides.

[ ] $\overset{?}{=}$ [ ] $\overset{?}{=}$ [ ]   Substitute the lengths of the sides.

[ ] = [ ] = [ ]   Simplify each ratio.

Since the ratios of the corresponding sides are [ ],

the triangles [ ] similar.

© Houghton Mifflin Harcourt Publishing Company

Holt McDougal Mathematics

Proportional Relationships

Similar Figures and Proportions, continued

Example 2

Tell whether the figures are similar.

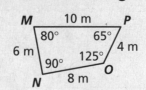

The [ ] angles of the

figures have [ ] measures.

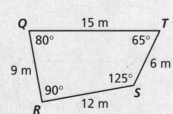

Write each set of [ ]

sides as a ratio.

[ ] $\overline{MN}$ corresponds to $\overline{QR}$.   [ ] $\overline{OP}$ corresponds to $\overline{ST}$.

[ ] $\overline{NO}$ corresponds to $\overline{RS}$.   [ ] $\overline{MP}$ corresponds to $\overline{QT}$.

Determine whether the ratios of the lengths of the corresponding sides

are [ ].

$$\frac{MN}{QR} \stackrel{?}{=} \frac{NO}{RS} \stackrel{?}{=} \frac{OP}{ST} \stackrel{?}{=} \frac{MP}{QT}$$

Write each ratio using the

[ ] sides.

$$\frac{6}{9} \stackrel{?}{=} \frac{8}{12} \stackrel{?}{=} \frac{4}{6} \stackrel{?}{=} \frac{10}{15}$$

Substitute the lengths of the sides.

[ ] = [ ] = [ ] = [ ]   Simplify each [ ].

The figures [ ] similar.

Check It Out!

1. Tell whether the triangles are similar.

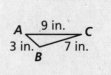 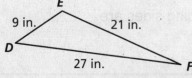

© Houghton Mifflin Harcourt Publishing Company

Holt McDougal Mathematics

Proportional Relationships
Using Similar Figures

Lesson Objectives

Use similar figures to find unknown measures

Vocabulary

indirect measurement _____

_____

Additional Examples

Example 1

Find the unknown measures in the similar figures.

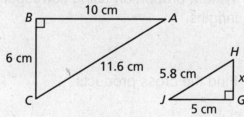

Find *x*.

$$\frac{GH}{BC} = \frac{JG}{BA}$$ Write a [_____] using corresponding [_____].

$$\frac{x}{\boxed{}} = \frac{\boxed{}}{10}$$ Substitute the lengths of the [_____].

$$10 \cdot x = \boxed{} \cdot \boxed{}$$ Find the [_____] products.

$$10x = \boxed{}$$ Multiply.

$$\frac{10x}{\boxed{}} = \frac{30}{\boxed{}}$$ Divide each side by [__].

$$x = \boxed{}$$

© Houghton Mifflin Harcourt Publishing Company

Holt McDougal Mathematics

Proportional Relationships

Using Similar Figures, continued

Example 2

The inside triangle is similar in shape to the outside triangle. Find the length of the base of the inside triangle.

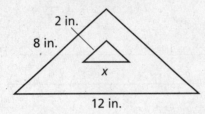

Let x = the [＿＿＿＿] of the base of the inside triangle.

$$\frac{\boxed{}}{\boxed{}} = \frac{\boxed{}}{x}$$ Write a proportion using corresponding side lengths.

$\boxed{} \cdot x = \boxed{} \cdot \boxed{}$ Find the cross products.

$\boxed{} \, x = \boxed{}$ Multiply.

$$\frac{\boxed{} \, x}{\boxed{}} = \frac{\boxed{}}{\boxed{}}$$ Divide each side by $\boxed{}$ to isolate the variable.

$x = \boxed{}$

The length of the base of the inside triangle is inches.

Holt McDougal Mathematics

© Houghton Mifflin Harcourt Publishing Company

Proportional Relationships

Using Similar Figures, continued

Example 3

City officials want to know the height of a traffic light. Estimate the height of the traffic light.

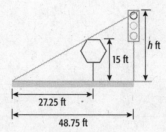

Write a [　　　　　　].

Use [　　　　　　] numbers to estimate.

Simplify.

Multiply each side by [　　] to isolate the variable.

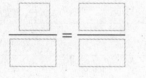

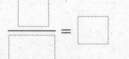

$h =$ [　　]

The height of the traffic light is about [　　] feet.

Check It Out!

1. $\triangle QRS \sim \triangle XYZ$. Find the unknown measures.

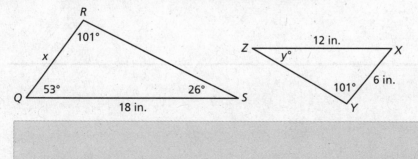

Holt McDougal Mathematics

© Houghton Mifflin Harcourt Publishing Company

Proportional Relationships
Scale Drawings and Scale Models

Lesson Objectives

Understand ratios and proportions in scale drawings; use ratios and proportions with scale

Vocabulary

scale drawing _____

_____

scale factor _____

_____

scale model _____

_____

scale _____

_____

Additional Examples

Example 1

Identify the scale factor.

	Room	Blueprint
Length (in.)	144	18
Width (in.)	108	13.5

$\dfrac{\text{blueprint length}}{\text{room length}} = \boxed{}$ Write a $\boxed{}$ using one of

the dimensions.

$= \boxed{}$ Simplify.

The scale factor is $\boxed{}$.

Holt McDougal Mathematics

© Houghton Mifflin Harcourt Publishing Company

Proportional Relationships

Scale Drawings and Scale Models, continued

Example 2

A photograph was enlarged and made into a poster. The poster is 20.5 inches by 36 inches. The scale factor is $\frac{5}{1}$. Find the size of the photograph.

Think: $\frac{\text{poster}}{\text{photo}} = \frac{5}{1}$

$\frac{36}{l} = \frac{5}{1}$ Write a [   ] to find the length l.

$5l = $ [   ]   Find the [   ] products.

$l = $ [   ]   Divide.

$\frac{20.5}{w} = \frac{5}{1}$ Write a [   ] to find the width w.

[   ] $w = $ [   ]   Find the cross [   ].

$w = $ [   ]   Divide.

The photo is in. long and [   ] in. wide.

Example 3

On a road map with a scale of 1.5 inches : 60 miles, the distance between Pittsburgh and Philadelphia is 7.5 inches. What is the actual distance between the two cities?

Let d be the actual distance between the cities.

[   ] $=$ [   ]   Write a proportion.

[   ] $\cdot d = $ [   ] $\cdot$ [   ]   Find the cross products.

[   ] $d = $ [   ]

© Houghton Mifflin Harcourt Publishing Company

Holt McDougal Mathematics

Proportional Relationships
Scale Drawings and Scale Models, continued

| | = | | Divide both sides by _____ .

$d =$ [_____]

The distance between the cities is [_____] miles.

Check It Out!

1. Identify the scale factor.

	Model Aircraft	Blueprint
Length (in.)	12	2
Wing span (in.)	18	3

2. Mary's father made her a dollhouse which was modeled after the blueprint of their home. The blueprint is 24 inches by 45 inches. The scale factor is $\frac{1.5}{1}$. Find the size of the dollhouse.

3. On a road map with a scale of 1 inch : 50 kilometers, the distance between Dallas and Houston is 7 inches. What is the actual distance between the two cities?

© Houghton Mifflin Harcourt Publishing Company

Holt McDougal Mathematics

Proportional Relationships
Chapter Review

1 Rates

Find each rate.

1. A lawn service company charges Mrs. Smith $75 for $2\frac{1}{2}$ hours of work. What is their fee per hour?

2. A chartered bus drove 650 miles in 13 hours. What was the average rate of speed of the bus?

2 Identifying and Writing Proportions

Determine whether the ratios are proportional.

3. $\frac{4}{8}, \frac{8}{10}$ 4. $\frac{2}{9}, \frac{10}{45}$ 5. $\frac{3}{5}, \frac{27}{45}$ 6. $\frac{11}{12}, \frac{22}{27}$

3 Solving Proportions

Use cross products to solve each proportion.

7. $\frac{4}{17} = \frac{y}{68}$ 8. $\frac{9}{x} = \frac{3}{7}$ 9. $\frac{p}{13} = \frac{33}{39}$ 10. $\frac{2}{9} = \frac{q}{54}$

11. Kathy walked 2.5 miles in 35 minutes. Use a proportion to find how long it would take her to walk 6 miles at the same speed.

© Houghton Mifflin Harcourt Publishing Company

Holt McDougal Mathematics

4 Similar Figures and Proportions

Use the properties of similarity to determine whether the figures are similar.

12.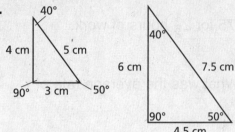

13.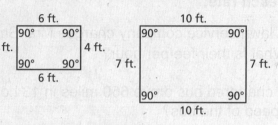

5 Using Similar Figures

14. Mrs. Nuss planted two similar rectangular gardens. Her soybean garden measures 100 yards long and 60 yards wide. Her corn garden is 150 yards long. How many yards wide is her corn garden?

15. Ned is 5 ft 4 in. tall, and casts a shadow that is 3 ft 6 in. long. At the same time his dad's tool shed casts a shadow that is 7 ft long. What is the height of the tool shed?

6 Scale Drawings and Scale Models

Identify the scale factor.

16.

	Library	Model
Height (ft)	56	4

17.

	Car	Model
Length (in.)	96	8

18. The map in Joe's World Atlas uses a scale of $\frac{1}{2}$ cm: 20 miles. On the map, the distance between Cleveland and Cincinnati is $5\frac{1}{2}$ cm.

What is the actual distance between the two cities?

© Houghton Mifflin Harcourt Publishing Company

Proportional Relationships

LESSON 4

Big Ideas

Answer these questions to summarize the important concepts from Chapter 4 in your own words.

1. Darin drove 245 miles in 5 hours. Explain how to find the unit rate.

2. Explain how to solve the proportion $\frac{14}{9} = \frac{x}{54}$ using cross products.

3. What is true about corresponding angles and corresponding sides of similar figures?

4. Two cities are 3.5 cm apart on a map. The scale factor is 2 cm = 25 miles. Explain how to find the actual distance d between the cities.

For more review of Chapter 4:

- Complete the Chapter 4 Study Guide and Review in your textbook.
- Complete the Ready to Go On quizzes in your textbook.

© Houghton Mifflin Harcourt Publishing Company

Holt McDougal Mathematics

Graphs
The Coordinate Plane

Lesson Objectives

Plot and identify ordered pairs on a coordinate plane

Vocabulary

coordinate plane _____

_____

x-axis _____

_____

y-axis _____

_____

origin _____

_____

quadrant _____

_____

ordered pair _____

_____

Additional Examples

Example 1

Identify the quadrant that contains each point.

A. S

S lies in Quadrant .

B. T

T lies in Quadrant .

C. W

W lies on the 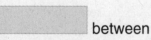 between

Quadrants [ ] and [ ].

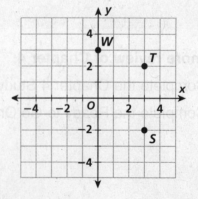

Holt McDougal Mathematics

© Houghton Mifflin Harcourt Publishing Company

Graphs

The Coordinate Plane, continued

Example 2

Plot each point on a coordinate plane.

A. *D* (3, 3)

Start at the ⬚. Move ⬚ units

right and ⬚ units up.

B. *E* (−2, −3)

Start at the ⬚. Move 2 units

⬚ and 3 units ⬚.

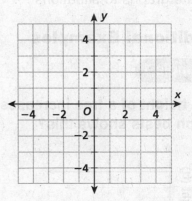

Example 3

Give the coordinates of the point.

X

Start at the ⬚. Point *X* is ⬚

units left and ⬚ units up. ▭

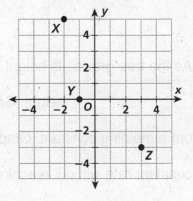

Check It Out!

1. Identify the quadrant that contains the point.

X

▭

2. Plot the point on the coordinate plane.

E (−2, 3)

3. Give the coordinates of the point.

L

▭

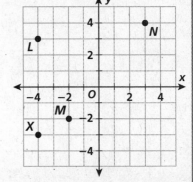

© Houghton Mifflin Harcourt Publishing Company

Holt McDougal Mathematics

Graphs
Interpreting Graphs

Lesson Objectives

Relate graphs to situations

Additional Examples

Example 1

The height of a tree increases over time, but not at a constant rate. Which graph bests shows this?

a.
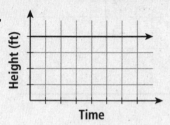

b.
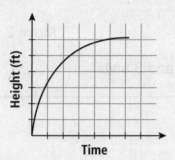

As the tree grows, its height [   ] and then reaches its

[   ] height. Graph [   ] shows the height of a tree not increasing

but remaining constant. Graph [   ] shows the height of a tree increasing at a

constant rate without reaching a maximum height. The answer is graph [   ].

© Houghton Mifflin Harcourt Publishing Company

Holt McDougal Mathematics

LESSON 2 **Graphs**

Interpreting Graphs, continued

Example 2 **PROBLEM SOLVING APPLICATION**

Jarod parked his car in the supermarket parking lot and walked 40 ft into the store to the customer service counter, where he waited in line to pay his electric bill. Jarod then walked 60 ft to the back of the store to get 2 gallons of milk and walked 50 ft to the checkout near the front of the store to pay for them. After waiting his turn and paying for the milk, he walked 50 ft back to his car. Sketch a graph to show Jarod's distance from his car over time. Use your graph to find the total distance traveled.

1. Understand the Problem

The answer is the [ ] Jarod traveled.

List the **important information**:

- Jarod walked to the [ ].

- Jarod [ ] in line.

- Jarod walked to the [ ] of the store.

- Jarod walked to the [ ].

- Jarod [ ] in line.

- Jarod went back to his [ ].

2. Make a Plan

Sketch a graph of the situation. Then use the graph to find the distance Jarod traveled.

3. Solve

The distance [ ] as Jarod walks to the customer service counter.

The distance [ ] when Jarod waits in line.

The distance [ ] as Jarod walks to the bar of the store.

© Houghton Mifflin Harcourt Publishing Company

83 Holt McDougal Mathematics

Graphs

Interpreting Graphs, continued

The distance _____ as Jarod walks to the checkout.

The distance _____ when Jarod waits in line.

The distance _____ as Jarod walks back to his car.

The distances increase from 0 to _____ and back to 0.

The total distance is _____ .

4. Look Back

The graph is reasonable because it pictures someone walking away, standing still, walking away, walking back, standing in line, and walking back. The distance is reasonable because Jarod was 100 ft away at his farthest point, then he returned to where he started.

Check It Out!

1. The dimensions of the basketball court have changed over the years. However, the height of the basket has not changed. Which graph bests shows this?

a.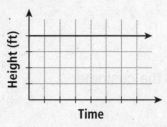

b.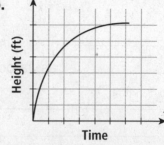

© Houghton Mifflin Harcourt Publishing Company

Holt McDougal Mathematics

Graphs
Slope and Rates of Change

Lesson Objectives

Determine the slope of a line and recognize constant and variable rates of change.

Vocabulary

slope _____

_____

rate of change _____

_____

Additional Examples

Example 1

Tell whether the slope is positive or negative. Then find the slope.

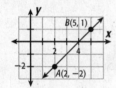

The line points [   ].

The slope is [   ].

slope = $\dfrac{\text{rise}}{\text{run}}$

= $\dfrac{}{}$ The rise is [   ]. The run is [   ].

= [   ]

© Houghton Mifflin Harcourt Publishing Company

Graphs
Slope and Rates of Change, continued

© Houghton Mifflin Harcourt Publishing Company

Example 2

Use the slope $\frac{-2}{1}$ and the point $(1, -1)$ to graph the line.

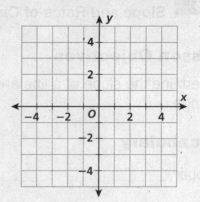

slope = $\frac{\text{rise}}{\text{run}}$ = $\dfrac{\boxed{}}{\boxed{}}$ or $\dfrac{\boxed{}}{\boxed{}}$

From the point $\boxed{}$, move $\boxed{}$ units down and $\boxed{}$ unit right, or

move $\boxed{}$ units up and $\boxed{}$ unit left. Mark the point where you end up, and draw a line through the two points.

Example 3

Tell whether the graph shows a constant or variable rate of change.

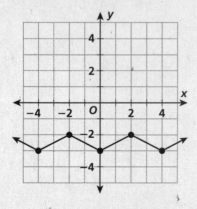

The graph is $\boxed{}$, so the

rate of change is $\boxed{}$.

Holt McDougal Mathematics

LESSON 3

Graphs

Slope and Rates of Change, continued

Example 4

The graph shows the distance a monarch butterfly travels over time. Tell whether the graph shows a constant or variable rate of change. Then find how fast the butterfly is traveling.

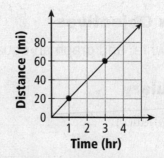

The graph is a line, so the butterfly is traveling

at a _____ rate of speed.

The amount of _____ is the rise, and the amount of _____

is the run. You can find the speed by finding the _____.

slope $= \dfrac{\boxed{}}{\boxed{}} = \dfrac{\boxed{} \text{ miles}}{\boxed{} \text{ hour}}$

The butterfly travels at a rate of _____ miles per hour.

Check It Out!

1. Tell whether the slope is positive or negative. Then find the slope.

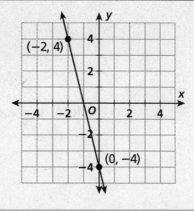

© Houghton Mifflin Harcourt Publishing Company

Holt McDougal Mathematics

Graphs
Direct Variation

Lesson Objectives

Identify, write, and graph an equation of direct variation

Vocabulary

direct variation _____

_____

constant of variation _____

_____

Additional Examples

Example 1

Tell whether each equation represents a direct variation. If so, identify the constant of variation.

A. $y + 8 = x$

$y + 8 = x$ Solve the equation for ☐. Subtract ☐ from both sides.

$y = x$ ☐

The equation ▆ in the form $y = kx$, so $y + 8 = x$ ▆ a direct variation.

B. $3y = 2x$

$\dfrac{3y}{☐} = \dfrac{2x}{☐}$ Solve the equation for ☐. Divide both sides by ☐.

$y = \dfrac{2}{☐}$ ☐

The equation ▆ in the form $y = kx$, so the original equation $3y = 2x$ ▆ a direct variation. The constant of variation is ▆.

Holt McDougal Mathematics

© Houghton Mifflin Harcourt Publishing Company

Graphs

Direct Variation, continued

© Houghton Mifflin Harcourt Publishing Company

Example 2

Tell whether each set of data represents a direct variation. If so, identify the constant of variation and then write the direct variation equation.

A.

Price ($)	69	99	129
Weight (oz)	2	3	4

Find $\frac{y}{x}$ for each ordered pair.

$\frac{y}{x} = \boxed{}$ $\qquad$ $\frac{y}{x} = \boxed{} = \boxed{}$ $\qquad$ $\frac{y}{x} = \boxed{}$

$k \boxed{}$ the same for each ordered pair.

The data $\boxed{}$ a direct variation.

Example 3

Tell whether the graph represents a direct variation. If so, identify the constant of variation and then write the direct variation equation.

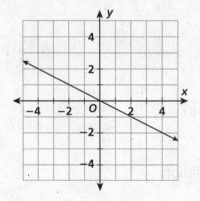

The graph is a line through ($\boxed{}$). This $\boxed{}$ a direct variation. The slope

of the line is $\boxed{}$, so $k = \boxed{}$. The equation is $y = \boxed{}$.

 Holt McDougal Mathematics

Graphs

Direct Variation, continued

Know it! Note

Example 4

A truck travels at a speed of 55 miles per hour.

A. Write a direct variation equation for the distance *y* the truck travels in *x* hours.

Use the formula $d = r \cdot t$, where *d* is distance, *r* is rate, and *t* is time.
rate = 55 miles per hour

$$\boxed{} = \boxed{} \cdot \boxed{}$$

B. Graph the data.

Make a table. Since time cannot be $\boxed{}$, use $\boxed{}$ $\boxed{}$ numbers for *x*.

x	y = 55x	y	(x, y)
0	y = 55($\boxed{}$)	$\boxed{}$	($\boxed{}$)
3	y = 55($\boxed{}$)	$\boxed{}$	($\boxed{}$)
6	y = 55($\boxed{}$)	$\boxed{}$	($\boxed{}$)

Use the ordered pairs to plot the points on a

coordinate plane. Connect the points in a straight

$\boxed{}$. Label the $\boxed{}$.

C. How long does it take the truck to travel 660 miles?

Find the value of *x* when $y = \boxed{}$.

$y = 55x$ Write the equation for the direct variation.

$\boxed{} = 55x$ Substitute $\boxed{}$ for *y*.

$\dfrac{660}{\boxed{}} = \dfrac{55x}{\boxed{}}$ Divide both sides by $\boxed{}$.

$\boxed{} = x$

It will take the truck $\boxed{}$ to travel 660 miles.

© Houghton Mifflin Harcourt Publishing Company

Holt McDougal Mathematics

Graphs

Direct Variation, continued

Check It Out!

1. Tell whether the equation $3y + 4x = 0$ represents a direct variation. If so, identify the constant of variation.

2. Tell whether the set of data represents a direct variation. If so, identify the constant of variation and then write the direct variation equation.

Price ($)	37.50	67.5	105
Tickets	5	9	14

© Houghton Mifflin Harcourt Publishing Company

Holt McDougal Mathematics

Graphs
Chapter Review

1 The Coordinate Plane

Identify the quadrant that contains each point.

1. (7, 3)

2. (−5, −1)

3. (−3, 0)

4. (2, −2)

Plot each ordered pair on a coordinate plane.

5. (3, −5)

6. (0, 4)

7. (−1, 6)

8. (4, 2)

2 Interpreting Graphs

9. An airplane increases in altitude from take-off until it reaches its cruising altitude. It flies at the cruising altitude until it begins to descend for landing. Which graph best shows the story?

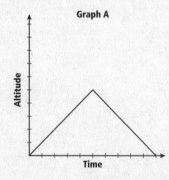

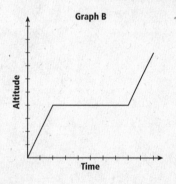

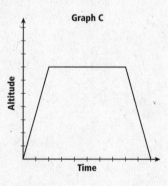

10. Nolan rode his bike 3 km to school. After school he rode his bike 4 km to a friend's house. Then he rode his bike home. Sketch a graph to show the distance Nolan traveled. Use the graph to find the distance Nolan traveled.

Possible answer:

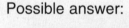

Holt McDougal Mathematics

© Houghton Mifflin Harcourt Publishing Company

3 Slope and Rates of Change

Use the given slope and point to graph each line.

11. $\frac{1}{3}$; (2, 2)

12. -2; (1, 0)

4 Direct Variation

Tell whether each equation represents a direct variation. If so, identify the constant of variation.

13. $-2y = 4x$

14. $3y = 6 - 8x$

15. $-5x + y = 0$

16. A car travels at a speed of 35 miles per hour. Write a direct variation equation for the distance y the car travels in x hours and graph the data. How long does it take the car to travel 96.25 miles?

© Houghton Mifflin Harcourt Publishing Company

Graphs

Big Ideas

Answer these questions to summarize the important concepts from Chapter 5 in your own words.

1. Explain how to plot the ordered pair $(4, -7)$.

2. Explain how to find the output value for the function $y = 6x + 2$ for $x = -5$.

3. Explain how to graph the solutions of the equation $y = 3x - 2$.

4. In the equation $y = 6x + 8$, which is the dependent variable and which is the independent variable? Explain.

For more review of Chapter 5:

- Complete the Chapter 5 Study Guide and Review in your textbook.
- Complete the Ready to Go On quizzes in your textbook.

© Houghton Mifflin Harcourt Publishing Company

Holt McDougal Mathematics

Percents
Fractions, Decimals, and Percents

Lesson Objectives

Write decimals and fractions as percents

Additional Examples

Example 1

Write 0.7 as a percent.

0.7 = ☐ = ☐   Write the decimal as fraction with a

denominator of ☐ .

= ☐ %   Write the ☐ with a
percent sign.

Example 2

Write $\frac{5}{8}$ as a percent.

$\frac{5}{8}$ = 5 ÷ 8   Use ☐ to write the
fraction as a decimal.

= ☐ = ☐ %   Write the decimal as a percent.

Example 3

Order 17%, 0.25, $\frac{3}{4}$, 0.1, $\frac{4}{5}$, and 20% from least to greatest.

Write the numbers as decimals with the same number of decimal places.

17% = ☐   0.25 = ☐ $\frac{3}{4}$ = ☐

0.1 = ☐ $\frac{4}{5}$ = ☐   20% = ☐

From least to greatest, the numbers are: ☐

© Houghton Mifflin Harcourt Publishing Company

Percents

Fractions, Decimals, and Percents, continued

Example 4

Decide whether using pencil and paper, mental math, or a calculator is most useful when solving the following problem. Then solve.

> If 27 out of 50 people surveyed have the newspaper delivered to their home, what percent of these people have the newspaper delivered to their home?

27 out of 50 = $\dfrac{\boxed{}}{\boxed{}}$

Think: Since the denominator is a factor

of 100, $\boxed{}$ is a good choice.

Use .

$\dfrac{27}{50} = \dfrac{27 \cdot 2}{50 \cdot 2} = \boxed{}$

Write an $\boxed{}$ fraction with a denominator of $\boxed{}$

= $\boxed{}$ %

Write the fraction as a percent.

Check It Out!

1. Write 0.01 as a percent.

2. Write $\dfrac{9}{60}$ as a percent.

3. Decide whether using pencil and paper, mental math, or a calculator is most useful when solving the following problem. Then solve.

   > If 18 out of 20 dentists recommend a certain brand of toothpaste, what percent of these dentists recommend the toothpaste?

© Houghton Mifflin Harcourt Publishing Company

Percents

Estimating with Percents

Lesson Objectives

Estimate percents

Additional Examples

Example 1

Use a fraction to estimate 27% of 63.

27% of 63 ≈ ☐ · 63   Think: 27% is about 25% and 25% is

equivalent to ☐

≈ ☐ · 60   Change 63 to a compatible number.

≈ ☐   Multiply.

27% of 63 is about ☐.

Example 2

Tara's T's is offering 2 T-shirts for $16, while Good-T's is running their buy one for $9.99, get one for half price sale. Which store offers the better deal?

First find the discount on the second T-shirt at Good T's.

50% of $9.99 = ☐ · $9.99   Think: 50% is equivalent to ☐.

≈ ☐ · $10   Change $9.99 to a compatible number.

≈ $☐   Multiply.

The discount is approximately $☐. Since $10 + $5 = $15, the cost of

two shirts at Good T's is about $☐.

The T-shirts at ☐ is a better deal.

Holt McDougal Mathematics

Percents

Estimating with Percents, continued

Example 3

Use 1% or 10% to estimate the percent of each number.

A. 4% of 18

18 is about 20, so find 4% of 20.

1% of 20 = $\boxed{}$

4% of 20 = 4 · $\boxed{}$ = $\boxed{}$ 4% equals $\boxed{}$ · 1%.

4% of 18 is about $\boxed{}$.

B. 29% of 80

29% is about 30, so find 30% of 80.

10% of 80 = $\boxed{}$

30% of 80 = 3 · $\boxed{}$ = $\boxed{}$ 30% equals $\boxed{}$ · 10%.

29% of 80 is about $\boxed{}$.

Example 4

Tim spent $58 on dinner for his family. About how much money should he leave for a 15% tip?

Since $58 is about $60, find 15% of $60.

15% = 10% + 5%   Think: 15% is 10% + 5%.

10% of $60 = $$\boxed{}$

5% of $60 = $6 ÷ 2 = $$\boxed{}$ 5% is $\frac{1}{2}$ of $\boxed{}$ % so divide $6 by 2.

$6 + $3 = $$\boxed{}$ $\boxed{}$ the 10% and 5% estimates.

Tim should leave about $$\boxed{}$ for a 15% tip.

© Houghton Mifflin Harcourt Publishing Company

Holt McDougal Mathematics

LESSON 2 — Percents
Estimating with Percents, continued

Check It Out!

1. Use a fraction to estimate 48% of 91.

2. Billy's Office Supply Store is offering 25% off a leather notebook, originally priced at $9.75. K's Office Supply Store offers the same notebook, not on sale, at $7.00. Which store offers the better deal?

3. Use 1% or 10% to estimate the percent of the number.

   21% of 60

4. Amanda spent $12 on a hair cut. About how much money should she leave for a 15% tip?

© Houghton Mifflin Harcourt Publishing Company

99

Holt McDougal Mathematics

Percents

Using Properties with Rational Numbers

Lesson Objective

Learn to use properties of rational numbers to write equivalent expressions and equations.

Additional Examples

Example 1

An art teacher pays $13.89 for one box of watercolor brushes. She buys 6 boxes in March and 5 boxes in April. Use the Distributive Property to write equivalent expressions showing two ways to calculate the total cost of the watercolor boxes.

Write an expression for total cost using the cost per box and the number of boxes. Then write an equivalent expression.

Cost per box	·	Total number of boxes	=	Cost per box	·	March boxes	+	Cost per box	·	April boxes

☐ · (6 + 5) = ☐ · ☐ + $13.89 · ☐

Simplify each expression to calculate the total cost.

Method 1

$13.89 · (☐ + ☐)

= $13.89 · 11

= ☐

Method 2

☐ · 6 + 13.89 · ☐

= ☐ + ☐

= ☐

Both methods result in a total cost of ☐ for the brushes.

Holt McDougal **Mathematics**

© Houghton Mifflin Harcourt Publishing Company

LESSON 3 **Percents**

Using Properties with Rational Numbers, continued

Example 2

Write an equivalent equation for $\frac{3}{4}x + 7 = \frac{5}{6}$ that does not contain fractions. Then solve the equation.

$$\frac{3}{4}x + 7 = \frac{5}{6}$$ The least common multiple of 4 and 6 is $\boxed{}$.

$\boxed{}\left(\frac{3}{4}x + 7\right) = \boxed{}\left(\frac{5}{6}\right)$ Multiply both sides by $\boxed{}$.

$\cancel{12}\left(\frac{3}{4}x\right) + 12(7) = \cancel{12}\left(\frac{5}{\cancel{6}}\right)$ Simplify to get an equivalent equation.

$9x + \boxed{} = \boxed{}$

$9x = -74$

$x = \boxed{}$ or $\boxed{}$ Solve for x.

Example 3

The soccer team uses a 36.75-liter container to take water to games. The team manager fills 0.75-liter bottles from this. He has used 22.5 liters. How many more 0.75-liter bottles can he fill before he runs out of water? Write and solve an equivalent equation without decimals.

$\boxed{}$ Write an equation to represent the situation.

$\boxed{}(0.75x + 22.5) = \boxed{}\,36.75$ The equation had decimals to the $\boxed{}$. Multiply both sides by $\boxed{}$.

$100(0.75x) + 100(22.5) = 100(36.75)$ Apply the $\boxed{}$ Property.

Simplify to get an equivalent equation.

$75x = \boxed{}$

$x = \boxed{}$ Solve for x.

The team manager can fill $\boxed{}$ more 0.75-liter bottles.

Holt McDougal Mathematics

Percents

Using Properties with Rational Numbers, continued

Check It Out!

1. Eli and Max each pay $3.75 for lunch using their lunch cards. Eli buys 8 lunches and Max buys 5 lunches. How much more does Eli pay than Max for the lunches?

2. Write an equivalent equation that does not contain fractions. Then solve the equation.

$$\frac{2}{7}x + 6 = \frac{1}{3}$$

3. Celia spent $11.80 on supplies for the pancake breakfast. She bought cartons of orange juice for $2.35 each and a large box of pancake mix for $4.75. How many cartons of orange juice did Celia buy? Write and solve an equivalent equation without decimals.

© Houghton Mifflin Harcourt Publishing Company

Holt McDougal Mathematics

Percents

Percent of Change

Lesson Objectives

Solve problems involving percent of change

Vocabulary

percent of change _____

_____

percent of increase _____

percent of decrease _____

Additional Examples

Example 1

Find each percent of change. Round answers to the nearest tenth of a percent, if necessary.

A. 65 is decreased to 38.

$65 - 38 =$ ☐   Find the amount of ☐.

percent of change $= \dfrac{27}{65}$ Substitute values into the formula.

≈ 0.4153846 Divide.

$\approx$ ☐ %   Write as a percent. Round.

The percent of decrease is about ☐ %.

B. 41 is increased to 92.

$92 - 41 =$ ☐   Find the amount of change.

Percent of change $= \dfrac{51}{41}$ Substitute values into the formula.

≈ 1.2439 Divide.

$\approx$ ☐ %   Write as a percent. Round.

The percent of increase is about ☐ %.

© Houghton Mifflin Harcourt Publishing Company

Percents
Percent of Change, continued

Example 2

The regular price of a bicycle helmet is $42.99. It is on sale for 20% off. What is the sale price?

Step 1: Find the amount of the discount.

$$20\% \cdot 42.99 = d \quad \text{Think: 20\% of \$42.99 is what number?}$$

$$\boxed{} \cdot 42.99 = d \quad \text{Write the percent as a decimal.}$$

$$\boxed{} = d$$

$$\$\boxed{} \approx d \quad \text{Round to the nearest cent.}$$

The discount is $\boxed{}$.

Step 2: Find the sale price.

regular price − amount of discount = sale price

$$\$42.99 - \$\boxed{} = \$\boxed{}$$

The sale price is $\boxed{}$.

Example 3

A boutique buys hand-painted T-shirts for $12.60 each and sells them at a 110% increase in price. What is the retail price of the T-shirts?

Step 1: Find the amount n of increase.
Think: 110% of $12.60 is what number?

$$110\% \cdot 12.60 = n$$

$$\boxed{} \cdot 12.60 = n \quad \text{Write the percent as a decimal.}$$

$$\boxed{} = n$$

The amount of increase is $\$\boxed{}$.

© Houghton Mifflin Harcourt Publishing Company

Holt McDougal Mathematics

Percents

Percent of Change, continued

Step 2: Find the selling price.

Think: retail price = wholesale price + amount of increase.

$p = \$12.60 + \$\boxed{}$

$p = \$\boxed{}$

The selling price of the hand-painted T-shirts is $\$\boxed{}$ each.

Check It Out!

1. **Find the percent of change. Round answers to the nearest tenth of a percent, if necessary.**

   70 is decreased to 45.

2. **The regular price of a computer game is $49.88. It is on sale for 15% off.**

   Find the sale price.

   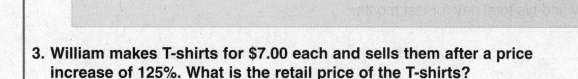

3. **William makes T-shirts for $7.00 each and sells them after a price increase of 125%. What is the retail price of the T-shirts?**

© Houghton Mifflin Harcourt Publishing Company

Holt McDougal Mathematics

LESSON 5 **Percents**

Applications of Percents

Lesson Objectives

Find commission, sales tax, and percent of earnings

Vocabulary

commission _____

_____

commission rate _____

_____

Additional Examples

Example 1

A real-estate agent is paid a monthly salary of $900 plus commission. Last month he sold one condominium for $65,000, earning a 4% commission on the sale. How much was his commission? What was his total pay last month?

First find his commission.

4% · $ [   ] = c   commission rate · sales = commission

0.04 · [   ] = c   Change the percent to a decimal.

[   ] = c   Solve for c.

He earned a commission of $ [   ] on the sale.

Now find his total pay for last month.

$ [   ] + $ [   ] = $ [   ]   commission + salary = total pay

His total pay for last month was $ [   ].

© Houghton Mifflin Harcourt Publishing Company

Holt McDougal Mathematics

Percents

Applications of Percents, continued

Example 2

If the sales tax rate is 6.75%, how much tax would Adrian pay if he bought two CDs at $16.99 each and one DVD for $36.29?

CD: 2 at $16.99 ———→ $ [   ]

DVD: 1 at $36.29 ———→ $ [   ]

$ [   ]   Total price

$0.0675 \cdot 70.27 = 4.743225$ Convert tax rate to a decimal and multiply by the total price.

Adrian would pay $ [   ] in sales tax.

Example 3

Anna earns $1500 monthly. Of that, $114.75 is withheld for Social Security and Medicare. What percent of Anna's earnings are withheld for Social Security and Medicare?

Think: What percent of $ [   ] is $114.75?

Solve by proportion:

$$\frac{n}{[\quad]} = \frac{114.75}{[\quad]}$$

$n \cdot$ [   ] = [   ] $\cdot 114.75$ Find the cross products.

[   ] = [   ]   Divide both sides by [   ]

$n =$ [   ]

$n =$ [   ]

[   ] % of Anna's earnings is withheld for Social Security and Medicare.

© Houghton Mifflin Harcourt Publishing Company

Holt McDougal Mathematics

Percents

Simple Interest

Know it!
Note

Lesson Objectives

Compute simple interest

Vocabulary

interest _____

simple interest _____

_____

principal _____

rate of interest _____

Additional Examples

Example 1

To buy a car, Jessica borrowed $15,000 for 3 years at an annual simple interest rate of 9%. How much interest will she pay if she pays the entire loan off at the end of the third year? What is the total amount that she will repay?

First, find the interest she will pay.

$I = P \cdot r \cdot t$ Use the formula.

$I = \boxed{} \cdot \boxed{} \cdot \boxed{}$ Substitute. Use 0.09 for 9%.

$I = \boxed{}$ Solve for I.

Jessica will pay $\$\boxed{}$ in interest.

You can find the total amount A to be repaid on a loan by adding the principal P to the interest I.

$P + I = A$ principal + interest = amount

$\boxed{} + \boxed{} = A$ Substitute.

$\boxed{} = A$ Solve for A.

Jessica will repay a total of $\$\boxed{}$ on her loan.

© Houghton Mifflin Harcourt Publishing Company

     Holt McDougal Mathematics

Percents
Simple Interest, continued

Example 2

Nancy invested $6000 in a bond at a yearly simple interest rate of 3%. She earned $450 in interest. How long was the money invested?

$I = P \cdot r \cdot t$ Use the formula.

$\boxed{} = \boxed{} \cdot \boxed{} \cdot t$ Substitute.

$\boxed{} = \boxed{}\,t$ Simplify.

$\boxed{} = t$ Solve for t.

The money was invested for $\boxed{}$ years, or $\boxed{}$ years $\boxed{}$ months.

Example 3

John's parents deposited $1000 into a savings account as a college fund when he was born. How much will John have in his account after 18 years at a yearly simple interest rate of 3.25%?

$I = P \cdot r \cdot t$ Use the formula.

$I = \boxed{} \cdot \boxed{} \cdot 18$ Substitute. Use $\boxed{}$ for 3.25%

$I = \boxed{}$ Solve for I.

Now you can find the total.

$P + I = A$ Use the formula.

$\boxed{} + \boxed{} = A$ Substitute.

$\boxed{} = A$ Solve for A.

John will have $\boxed{}$ in his college fund after 18 years.

© Houghton Mifflin Harcourt Publishing Company

Percents
Simple Interest, continued

Example 4

Mr. Johnson borrowed $8000 for 4 years to make home improvements. If he repaid a total of $10,320, at what interest rate did he borrow the money?

$$P + I = A$$ Use the formula.

$$\boxed{} + I = \boxed{}$$

$$I = 10{,}320 - 8000 = \boxed{}$$ Find the amount of interest.

He paid $\boxed{}$ in interest. Use the amount of interest to find the interest rate.

$$I = P \cdot r \cdot t$$ Use the formula.

$$\boxed{} = \boxed{} \cdot r \cdot \boxed{}$$ Substitute.

$$\boxed{} = \boxed{} \cdot r$$ Multiply.

$$\frac{2320}{\boxed{}} = r$$ Divide both sides by 32,000.

$$\boxed{} = r$$

Mr. Johnson borrowed the money at an annual rate of %, or $\boxed{}$%.

Check It Out!

1. To buy a laptop computer, Elaine borrowed $2000 for 3 years at an annual simple interest rate of 5%. How much interest will she pay if she pays the entire loan off at the end of the third year? What is the total amount that she will repay?

2. Laura invested $7500 in a bond at a yearly rate of 1.5%. She earned $450 in interest. How long was the money invested?

© Houghton Mifflin Harcourt Publishing Company

Holt McDougal Mathematics

LESSON 6

Percents

Chapter Review

Know it! Note

1 Fractions, Decimals, and Percents

Write each decimal as a percent.

1. 0.37

2. 0.045

3. 0.05

4. 0.627

5. Sam asked 20 friends if they liked peanut butter and jelly sandwiches or grilled cheese sandwiches. Thirteen of his friends said peanut butter and jelly. What percent liked peanut butter and jelly?

2 Estimating with Percents

Use a fraction to estimate the percent of each number.

6. 19% of 61

7. 76% of 62

8. 49% of 98

9. 19% of 86

Estimate.

10. 15% of $41.07

11. 32% of 211

12. 1% of 95

13. Alex has $15.00. He finds an item on sale for 20% off the regular price of $19.99. Does he have enough money to buy the toy? Explain.

3 Using Properties with Rational Numbers

Write an equivalent equation that does not contain fractions or decimals. Then solve the equation.

14. $\frac{3}{5}x + 1 = 3$

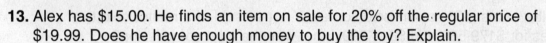

© Houghton-Mifflin Harcourt Publishing Company

Holt McDougal Mathematics

15. $0.5m + 1.5 = 2.5$

4 Percent of Change

Find each percent of change. Round answers to the nearest tenth of a percent, if necessary.

16. 150 to 220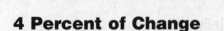

17. 37 to 31

18. A store buys milk from a dairy for $1.90 a gallon. They sell it to their customers for $2.29 a gallon. What percent increase is this?

5 Applications of Percents

Find each commission or sales tax to the nearest cent.

19. total sales: $16,000
commission: 3.75%

20. total sales: $21,500
sales tax: 6.75%

21. A realtor earns a 3% commission on each house sold. If a realtor sold two houses for $179,500 and $214,000, what was the total commission?

22. A car salesman earned $918.75 from a commission rate of 3.75% on the sale of a car. What was the price of the car?

6 Simple Interest

Find the interest and total amount to the nearest tenth.

23. $650 at 4.5% per year for 4 years

24. $2,250 at 3% per year for 2 years

25. John borrowed $25,000 to fix his porch. The bank charged him a simple interest rate of 7.75%. How much will John owe if he pays the bank back in 5 years?

© Houghton Mifflin Harcourt Publishing Company

Percents
Big Ideas

Answer these questions to summarize the important concepts from this Chapter 6 in your own words.

1. Explain how to write 45% as a fraction.

2. Explain how to find 150% of 350.

3. Explain how to find the interest rate when the simple interest is $360, the principal is $1,600, and the time is 6 years.

For more review of Chapter 6:

• Complete the Chapter 6 Study Guide and Review in your textbook.

• Complete the Ready to Go On quizzes in your textbook.

© Houghton Mifflin Harcourt Publishing Company

Collecting, Displaying, and Analyzing Data
Mean, Median, Mode, and Range

Lesson Objectives

Find the mean, median, mode, and range of a data set

Vocabulary

mean _____

_____

median _____

_____

mode _____

_____

range _____

_____

outlier _____

_____

© Houghton Mifflin Harcourt Publishing Company

Holt McDougal Mathematics

Collecting, Displaying, and Analyzing Data

Mean, Median, Mode, and Range, continued

Additional Examples

Example 1

Find the mean, median, mode, and range of the data set.

4, 7, 8, 2, 1, 2, 4, 2

mean:

$4 + 7 + 8 + 2 + 1 + 2 + 4 + 2 = 30$ Add the values.

$30 \div 8 = \boxed{}$ Divide the sum by the

_____.

The mean is ▨.

median:

1, 2, 2, 2, 4, 4, 7, 8   Arrange the values in order.

$2 + 4 = 6$ Since there are two middle values, find the

$6 \div 2 = \boxed{}$ _____ of these two values.

The median is ▨.

mode:

1, 2, 2, 2, 4, 4, 7, 8   The value occurs three times.

The mode is ▨.

range:

1, 2, 2, 2, 4, 4, 7, 8   _____ the least value from the

$8 - 1 = \boxed{}$ greatest value.

The range is ▨.

© Houghton Mifflin Harcourt Publishing Company

Holt McDougal Mathematics

Collecting, Displaying, and Analyzing Data

Mean, Median, Mode, and Range, continued

Example 2

The line plot shows the number of miles each of the 17 members of the cross-country team ran in a week. Which measure of central tendency best describes these data? Justify your answer.

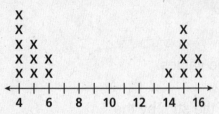

mean:

$$\frac{4 + 4 + 4 + 4 + 4 + 5 + 5 + 5 + 6 + 6 + 14 + 15 + 15 + 15 + 15 + 16 + 16}{17}$$

$= \dfrac{153}{17} = \boxed{}$

The $\boxed{}$ best describes the data set because the data is $\boxed{}$ fairly evenly about two areas.

median: 4, 4, 4, 4, 4, 5, 5, 5, 6, 6, 14, 15, 15, 15, 15, 16, 16

The median is $\boxed{}$.

The median $\boxed{}$ best describe the data set because many values are

not $\boxed{}$ around the data value $\boxed{}$.

mode:

The greatest number of X's occur above the number $\boxed{}$ on the line plot.

The mode is $\boxed{}$.

The mode focuses on one data value and does not describe the data set.

© Houghton Mifflin Harcourt Publishing Company

Holt McDougal Mathematics

Collecting, Displaying, and Analyzing Data

Mean, Median, Mode, and Range, continued

Example 3

The data shows Sara's scores for the last 5 math tests: 88, 90, 55, 94, and 89. Identify the outlier in the data set. Then determine how the outlier affects the mean, median, and mode of the data. Then tell which measure of central tendency best describes the data with the outlier.

The outlier is [ ].

Without the Outlier

mean:

$$\frac{88 + 89 + 90 + 94}{4} = \frac{361}{4} = \boxed{}$$

median:

88, [ ], 90, 94

$$\frac{89 + 90}{2} = \boxed{}$$

The median is [ ].

mode:

There is no [ ].

With the Outlier

mean:

$$\frac{55 + 88 + 89 + 90 + 94}{5} = \frac{416}{5} = \boxed{}$$

median:

55, 88, [ ], 90, 94

The median is [ ].

mode:

There is no [ ].

Adding the outlier [   ] the mean by [   ] and the

[   ] by 0.5.

There is no [   ] with or without the outlier. The [   ] best describes the data with the outlier.

Check It Out!

1. Find the mean, median, mode, and range of the data set.
   6, 4, 3, 5, 2, 5, 1, 8

Holt McDougal Mathematics

© Houghton Mifflin Harcourt Publishing Company

Collecting, Displaying, and Analyzing Data

Box-and-Whisker Plots

Lesson Objectives

Display and analyze data in box-and-whisker plots

Vocabulary

box-and-whisker plot _____

_____

lower quartile _____

_____

upper quartile _____

_____

interquartile range _____

_____

Additional Examples

Example 1

Use the data to make a box-and-whisker plot.

Heights of Basketball Players (in.)

73, 67, 75, 81, 67, 75, 85, 69

Step 1: Order the data from least to greatest. Then find the least and

greatest [_____], the [_____], and the upper and lower

[_____].

67 67 69 73 75 75 81 85   Find the lower and upper [_____].

67 67 69 $\frac{73 + 75}{2}$ 75 81 85   Find the [_____].

= [_____]

67 67 69 73 | 75 75 81 85   Find the lower and upper quartiles.

Holt McDougal Mathematics

© Houghton Mifflin Harcourt Publishing Company

Collecting, Displaying, and Analyzing Data

Box-and-Whisker Plots, continued

first quartile = $\dfrac{67 + 69}{2}$ = ⬚

third quartile = $\dfrac{75 + 81}{2}$ = ⬚

Step 2: Draw a number line.

Above the number line, plot a point for each value in Step 1.

Step 3: Draw a box from the ⬚ and ⬚ quartiles.

Inside the box, draw a vertical line through the ⬚.

Then draw the ⬚ from the box to the least and greatest values.

Example 2

Use the box-and-whisker plot in Additional Example 1 and the one below to answer each question.

Heights of Baseball Players (in.)

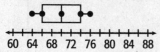

60 64 68 72 76 80 84 88

A. Which set of heights of players has the greater median?

The median of the heights of the ⬚ players, about

⬚, is greater than the median of the heights of the

⬚ players, about ⬚.

© Houghton Mifflin Harcourt Publishing Company

Holt McDougal Mathematics

Collecting, Displaying, and Analyzing Data

Box-and-Whisker Plots, continued

Use the box-and-whisker plot in Additional Example 1 and the one below to answer each question.

Heights of Baseball Players (in.)

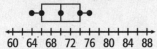

60 64 68 72 76 80 84 88

B. Which players have a greater interquartile range?

The length of the [____] in a box-and-whisker plot indicates the

[____] range. [____] has a longer

box, so it has a greater interquartile range.

C. Which group of players has more predictability in their height?

The [____] and [____] are smaller for

[____] players, which means that there is less variation in the

data. So the heights of [____] players is more predictable.

Check It Out!

1. Use the data to make a box-and-whisker plot.

42, 22, 31, 27, 24, 38, 35

2. Use the box-and-whisker plots below to answer the question.

Which shoe store has a greater interquartile range?

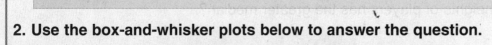

Maroon's Shoe Store

Sage's Shoe Store

20 22 24 26 28 30 32 34 36 38 40 42 44

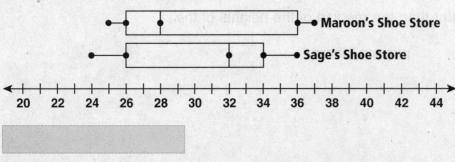

© Houghton Mifflin Harcourt Publishing Company

Holt McDougal Mathematics

Collecting, Displaying, and Analyzing Data
Populations and Samples

Lesson Objectives

Compare and analyze sampling methods

Vocabulary

population _____

_____

sample _____

random sample _____

_____

convenience sample _____

_____

biased sample _____

Additional Examples

Example 1

Determine which sampling method will better represent the entire population. Justify your answer.

Band Uniform Style

Sampling method	Results
Maria surveys only the band students she knows personally.	84% want blue uniforms
Jon writes each band student's name on a card. He questions those students whose name he draws.	61% want blue uniforms

_____ method produces results that better represent the entire band

population because he uses a _____ sample.

_____ method produces results that are not as representative of the

entire band population because she uses a _____
sample.

© Houghton Mifflin Harcourt Publishing Company

Collecting, Displaying, and Analyzing Data

Populations and Samples, continued

Example 2

Determine whether each sample may be biased. Explain.

A. The mayor surveys 100 supporters at a rally about the most important issues to be addressed by the city council.

The sample [____] biased. It is likely that the supporters may have

[_____] ideas than those not at the rally.

B. The principal sends out questionnaires to all of the students to find out what kind of music students prefer at dances.

The sample [_____] biased. It is [_____] because

[_____] student has a chance to respond.

Example 3

A principal of a school with 1,500 students estimates that about 400 students will attend a band festival on Saturday. A random sample of 25 students showed that 6 of them will attend. Determine whether the principal's estimate is likely to be accurate.

Set up a proportion to predict the total number of students that will attend.

$$\frac{\text{students attending in sample}}{\text{size of sample}} = \frac{\text{students attending in population}}{\text{size of population}}$$

$\dfrac{[\ ]}{[\ ]} = \dfrac{x}{[\ ]}$ Let x represent the number of students that will attend the band festival.

$6 \cdot 1{,}500 = 25 \cdot x$ The cross products are equal.

$[\ ] = 25x$ Multiply.

$\dfrac{9{,}000}{[\ ]} = \dfrac{25x}{[\ ]}$ Divide each side by $[\ ]$.

$[\ ] = x$

Based on the sample, you can predict that [_____] students will attend

the band festival. The principal's estimate [_____] to be accurate.

© Houghton Mifflin Harcourt Publishing Company

Holt McDougal Mathematics

Collecting, Displaying, and Analyzing Data

Populations and Samples, continued

Check It Out!

1. Determine which sampling method will better represent the entire population. Justify your answer.

Sampling Method	Results
Pedro surveys the offense on his football team on who was the team's most valuable player	87% said the quarterback was the most valuable player.
Chad surveys 5 players from the offense and 5 players from the defense on his football team on who was the team's most valuable player	65% said the quarterback was the most valuable player.

2. Determine whether the sample may be biased. Explain.

The owner of a record shop surveys only customers over the age of 18 who shop at his store.

3. The owner of a large chain restaurant with 1,200 employees estimates that about 250 employees will ask for winter vacation. A random sample of 40 employees showed that 8 of them will ask for the time off. Determine whether the owner's estimate is likely to be accurate.

© Houghton Mifflin Harcourt Publishing Company

Holt McDougal Mathematics

Collecting, Displaying, and Analyzing Data
Chapter Review

Know it!
Note

1 Mean, Median, Mode, and Range

The list shows the ages of men on a tennis team.

23, 40, 42, 34, 31, 36, 49, 58, 25, 36, 28

1. Find the mean, median, and mode, and range of the data. Round your answers to the nearest tenth of a year.

2. Which measure of central tendency best represents the data? Explain.

2 Box-and-Whisker Plots

3. Make a box-and-whisker plot of the data.

   29, 25, 21, 20, 17, 16, 15, 33, 33, 30, and 15.

4. Use the box-and-whisker plot you made in Exercise 10. How many numbers are greater than the upper quartile?

3 Populations and Samples

Determine whether each sample may be biased. Explain.

5. A school principal randomly chooses 75 students for a survey on the cafeteria food.

6. A reporter surveys 120 people leaving a baseball game to find out their favorite baseball team.

© Houghton Mifflin Harcourt Publishing Company

Holt McDougal Mathematics

Collecting, Displaying, and Analyzing Data

Big Ideas

Answer these questions to summarize the important concepts from Chapter 7 in your own words.

1. Explain how to find the mean, median, mode, and range of the data set.

   5, 8, 10, 12, 6, 5, 3

2. Give an example of a biased sample and explain why it is biased.

3. Explain the difference between sample and population.

For more review of Chapter 7:

• Complete the Chapter 7 Study Guide and Review in your textbook.

• Complete the Ready to Go On quizzes in your textbook.

© Houghton Mifflin Harcourt Publishing Company

Holt McDougal Mathematics

Geometric Figures

Building Blocks of Geometry

Lesson Objectives

Identify and describe geometric figures

Vocabulary

point _____

line _____

_____

plane _____

_____

ray _____

line segment _____

_____

congruent _____

_____

Additional Examples

Example 1

Identify the figures in the diagram.

A. three points [   ]

B. two lines [   ]   Choose any [   ] points on a line to name the line.

C. a plane [   ]   Choose any [   ] points, not on the same line, in any order.

© Houghton Mifflin Harcourt Publishing Company

Holt McDougal Mathematics

Geometric Figures
Building Blocks of Geometry, continued

Example 2

Identify the figures in the diagram.

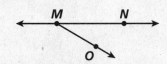

A. three rays

[ ] Name the [ ] of a ray first.

B. two line segments

[ ] Use the [ ] in any order to name a
segment.

Example 3

Identify the line segments that are congruent
in the figure.

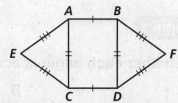

 ≅ [ ]   One tick

mark

[ ] ≅ [ ]   Two tick marks

 ≅ [ ] ≅ [ ]   Three tick marks

Check It Out!

1. Identify two lines in the figure.

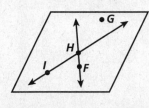

[ ]

Holt McDougal Mathematics

© Houghton Mifflin Harcourt Publishing Company

Geometric Figures

Classifying Angles

Lesson Objectives

Identify angles and angle pairs

Vocabulary

angle _____

vertex _____

right angle _____

acute angle _____

obtuse angle _____

straight angle _____

complementary angles _____

supplementary angles _____

Example 1

Tell whether each angle is acute, right, obtuse, or straight.

A.

B.

[   ] angle   [   ] angle

Holt McDougal Mathematics

© Houghton Mifflin Harcourt Publishing Company

Geometric Figures
Classifying Angles, continued

Additional Examples

Example 2

Use the diagram to tell whether the angles are complementary, supplementary, or neither.

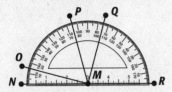

A. ∠*OMP* and ∠*PMQ*

m∠*OMP* = [ ]° and m∠*PMQ* = [ ]°

Since [ ]° + [ ]° = [ ]° , ∠*OMP* and ∠*PMQ* are

[   ].

Example 3

Angles *A* and *B* are complementary. If m∠*A* is 56°, what is m∠*B*?

m∠*A* + m∠*B* = 90°

[ ]° + m∠*B* = 90° Substitute [ ]° for m∠*A*.

−56° −56° Subtract [ ]° from both sides to isolate m∠[ ].

m∠*B* = [ ]°

The m∠*B* is [ ]° .

Check It Out!

1. Tell whether the angle is acute, right, obtuse, or straight.

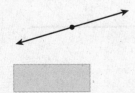

© Houghton Mifflin Harcourt Publishing Company

Holt McDougal Mathematics

Geometric Figures

Line and Angle Relationships

Lesson Objectives

Identify parallel, perpendicular, and skew lines, and angles formed by a transversal

Vocabulary

perpendicular lines _____

parallel lines _____

skew lines _____

_____

adjacent angles _____

_____

vertical angles _____

transversal _____

Example 1

Tell whether the lines appear parallel, perpendicular, or skew.

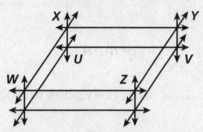

A. $\overleftrightarrow{UV}$ and $\overleftrightarrow{YV}$

$\overleftrightarrow{UV}$ ▨ $\overleftrightarrow{YV}$

The lines appear to intersect to form

☐ angles.

B. $\overleftrightarrow{XU}$ and $\overleftrightarrow{WZ}$

$\overleftrightarrow{XU}$ and $\overleftrightarrow{WZ}$ are ▨

The lines are in different planes and

do not ☐.

© Houghton Mifflin Harcourt Publishing Company

Holt McDougal Mathematics

Geometric Figures
Line and Angle Relationships, continued

Additional Examples

Example 2

Line *n* ∥ line *p*. Find the measure of each angle.

A. ∠2

∠2 and the 130° angle are [   ]

angles. Since [   ] angles are

congruent, m∠2 = [   ]°.

B. ∠3

∠3 and the 50° angle are [   ] angles. Since

[   ] angles are congruent, m∠3 = [   ]°.

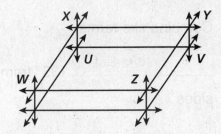

Check It Out!

1. Tell whether the lines appear parallel, perpendicular, or skew.

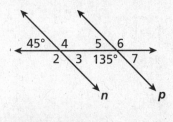

$\overrightarrow{WX}$ and $\overleftrightarrow{ZY}$ [   ]

2. Line *n* ∥ line *p*. Find the measure of ∠4.

[   ]

© Houghton Mifflin Harcourt Publishing Company

Holt McDougal Mathematics

Geometric Figures

Angles in Polygons

Lesson Objectives

Find the measures of angles in polygons

Vocabulary

diagonal _____

_____

Additional Examples

Find the unknown measure in the triangle.

55°
80°   x

$80° + 55° + x = \boxed{}°$ The sum of the measures of the

angles is $\boxed{}°$.

$135° + x = \boxed{}°$ Combine like terms.

$-\boxed{}°$ $-\boxed{}°$ $\boxed{}°$ 135° from both

sides.

$x = \boxed{}°$

The measure of the unknown angle is .

© Houghton Mifflin Harcourt Publishing Company

Geometric Figures

Angles in Polygons, continued

Example 2

Find the unknown angle measure in the quadrilateral.

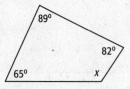

$65° + 89° + 82° + x = $ ☐°   The sum of the measures of the angles

is ☐° .

$236° + x = $ ☐°   Combine like terms.

$-236°$ $-236°$ ☐   236° from both sides.

$x = $ ☐°

The measure of the unknown angle is ▨° .

Example 3

Divide the polygon into triangles to find the sum of its angle measures.

A.

☐ · 180° = ☐°   There are ☐ triangles.

The sum of the angle measures of an octagon is ▨° .

Check It Out!

1. Find the unknown measure in the triangle.

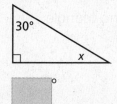

▨°

© Houghton Mifflin Harcourt Publishing Company

Holt McDougal Mathematics

LESSON 5

Geometric Figures
Congruent Figures

Lesson Objectives

Identify congruent figures and use congruence to solve problems

Vocabulary

Side-Side-Side Rule _____

_____

Additional Examples

Example 1

Identify any congruent figures.

The sides of the octagons [_____] congruent. Each side of the

outer figure is larger than each side of the inner figure.

Example 2

Determine whether the triangles are congruent.

$AB =$ [___] cm $PQ =$ [___] cm

$BC =$ [___] cm $PR =$ [___] cm

$AC =$ [___] cm $RQ =$ [___] cm

The triangles [_____] congruent. Although two sides in one triangle

[_____] congruent to two sides in the other, the third sides

[_____] congruent.

Holt McDougal Mathematics

© Houghton Mifflin Harcourt Publishing Company

Example 3

Determine the unknown measures in the set of congruent polygons.

A.
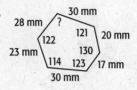

The corresponding angles are

[   ].

The unknown angle measure is [   ]°.

B.
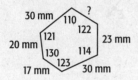

The corresponding sides are

[   ].

The unknown side length is [   ] mm.

Check It Out!

1. Determine whether the triangles are congruent.

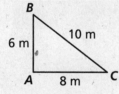 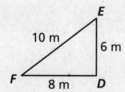

2. Determine the unknown measures in the set of congruent polygons.

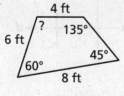

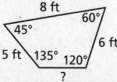

© Houghton Mifflin Harcourt Publishing Company

Geometric Figures

Chapter Review

Know it!
Note

1 Building Blocks of Geometry

Identify the figures in the diagram.

1. three points

2. two lines

3. a plane

4. three rays

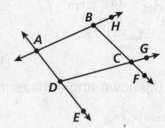

2 Classifying Angles

Classify each pair of angles as complementary or supplementary. Then find the missing angle measure.

5.

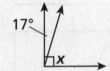

17°

x

6.

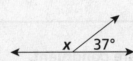

x   37°

7.

129°
x

3 Line and Angle Relationships

For Exercises 9-12, use the figure to complete each statement.

8. Lines *a* and *d* are ___?___ .

9. Lines *b* and *a* are ___?___ .

10. ∠1 and ∠5 are ___?___ . They are also ___?___ .

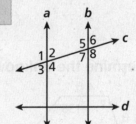

© Houghton Mifflin Harcourt Publishing Company

Geometric Figures

Chapter Review, continued

4 Angles in Polygons

Find the measure of the third angle in each triangle, given two angle measures. Then classify the triangle.

11. 36°, 19° [   ]   **12.** 61°, 52° [   ]

5 Congruent Figures

Determine the missing measures in each set of congruent polygons.

13.

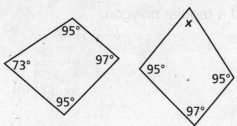

14.

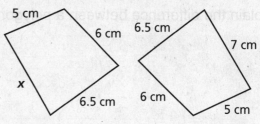

Holt McDougal Mathematics

© Houghton Mifflin Harcourt Publishing Company

Geometric Figures

Big Ideas

Answer these questions to summarize the important concepts from Chapter 8 in your own words.

1. Explain the difference between complementary and supplementary angles.

2. Explain the difference between a polygon and a regular polygon.

3. Two angle measures in a triangle are 35° and 77°. Explain how to find the third angle measure in the triangle.

4. Explain how to determine if two polygons are congruent.

For more review of Chapter 8:

- Complete the Chapter 8 Study Guide and Review in your textbook.
- Complete the Ready to Go On quizzes in your textbook.

© Houghton Mifflin Harcourt Publishing Company

Measurement and Geometry
Perimeter and Circumference

Know it! Note

Lesson Objectives

Find the perimeter of a polygon and the circumference of a circle

Vocabulary

perimeter _____

_____

circumference _____

_____

pi _____

_____

Additional Examples

Example 1

Find the perimeter of the polygon.

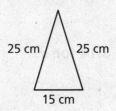
25 cm   25 cm

15 cm

$P =$ ☐ $+$ ☐ $+$ ☐   Use the side lengths.

$P =$ ☐   Add.

The perimeter of the triangle is ☐ cm.

© Houghton Mifflin Harcourt Publishing Company

Example 2

Find the perimeter of the rectangle.

14 ft
18 ft

$P = 2l + 2w$ Use the formula.

$P = (2 \cdot \boxed{}) + (2 \cdot \boxed{})$ Substitute for l and w.

$P = \boxed{} + \boxed{}$ Multiply.

$P = \boxed{}$ Add.

The perimeter of the rectangle is ft.

Example 3

Find the circumference of each circle to the nearest tenth. Use 3.14 for π.

A.

12 in.

$C = \pi d$ You know the diameter.

$C \approx \boxed{} \cdot 12$ Substitute for π and d.

$C \approx \boxed{}$ Multiply.

The circumference of the circle is about [   ] in.

© Houghton Mifflin Harcourt Publishing Company

LESSON 1 — Measurement and Geometry

Perimeter and Circumference, continued

Example 4

The diameter of a circular pond is 42 m. What is its circumference?
Use $\frac{22}{7}$ for π.

$C = \pi d$	You know the diameter.
$C \approx \boxed{} \cdot 42$	Substitute $\boxed{}$ for π and 42 for d.
$C \approx \boxed{} \cdot \dfrac{42}{1}$	Write 42 as a fraction.
$C \approx \boxed{} \cdot \dfrac{42}{1}$	Simplify.
$C \approx \boxed{}$	Multiply.

The circumference of the pond is about _____ m.

Check It Out!

1. Find the perimeter of the polygon.

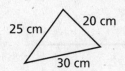

25 cm   20 cm   30 cm

2. Find the perimeter of the rectangle.

16 ft   8 ft

3. Find the circumference of the circle to the nearest tenth. Use 3.14 for π.

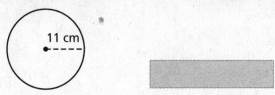

11 cm

4. The diameter of a circular spa is 14 m. What is its circumference?

Use $\frac{22}{7}$ for π.

© Houghton Mifflin Harcourt Publishing Company

Measurement and Geometry
Area of Circles

Lesson Objectives

Find the area of circles

Additional Examples

Example 1

Find the area of each circle to the nearest tenth. Use 3.14 for π.

A.

7 cm

$A = \pi r^2$ Use the formula.

$A \approx 3.14 \cdot \boxed{}^2$ Substitute $\boxed{}$ for r.

$A \approx 3.14 \cdot \boxed{}$ Evaluate the power.

$A \approx \boxed{}$ Multiply.

The area of the circle is about $\boxed{}$ cm².

Example 2

Park employees are fitting a top over a circular drain in the park. If the radius of the drain is 14 inches, what is the area of the top that will cover the drain? Use $\frac{22}{7}$ for π.

$A = \pi r^2$ Use the formula for the area of a circle.

$A \approx \frac{22}{7} \cdot \boxed{}^2$ Substitute. Use $\boxed{}$ for r.

$A \approx \frac{22}{7} \cdot \boxed{}$ Evaluate the power.

$A \approx 22 \cdot 28$

$A \approx \boxed{}$ Multiply.

The area of the top that will cover the drain is about $\boxed{}$ in².

© Houghton Mifflin Harcourt Publishing Company

Holt McDougal Mathematics

Example 3

Use a centimeter ruler to measure the radius of the circle. Then find the area of the shaded region of the circle. Use 3.14 for π. Round your answer to the nearest tenth.

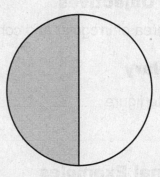

First measure the radius of the circle: It measures _____ cm.

Now find the area of the entire circle.

$A = \pi r^2$ Use the formula for the area of a circle.

$A \approx 3.14 \cdot \boxed{}^2$ Substitute. Use _____ for r.

$A \approx 3.14 \cdot \boxed{}$ Evaluate the power.

$A \approx \boxed{}$ Multiply.

$A \approx \boxed{}$

Since _____ of the circle is shaded, divide the area of the circle by _____.

The area of the shaded region of the circle is about _____ cm².

Check It Out!

1. Find the area of the circle to the nearest tenth. Use 3.14 for π.

12 ft

© Houghton Mifflin Harcourt Publishing Company

Measurement and Geometry
Area of Irregular Figures

Know it! Note

Lesson Objectives

Find the area of irregular and complex figures

Vocabulary

composite figure _____

_____

Additional Examples

Example 1

Estimate the area of the figure. Each square represents one square yard.

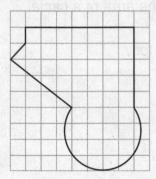

Count the number of filled or almost filled squares: ☐

Count the number of squares half-filled: ☐

Add the number of filled squares plus $\frac{1}{2}$ the number of half-filled squares:

☐ + ($\frac{1}{2}$ • ☐) = ☐ + ☐ = ▨ .

The area of the figure is about ▨ yds^2.

© Houghton Mifflin Harcourt Publishing Company

Holt McDougal Mathematics

Example 2

Find the area of the figure. Use 3.14 for π.

Step 1: Separate the figure into smaller, similar figures.

Step 2: Find the area of each smaller figure.
Area of the parallelogram:
$A = bh$

Use the formula for the area of a parallelogram.

$A = $ [ ] $\cdot$ [ ]

Substitute [ ] for b and [ ] for h.

$A = $ [ ]

Multiply.

Area of semicircle:
$A = \frac{1}{2}(\pi r^2)$

The area of a semicircle is $\frac{1}{2}$ the area of a circle.

$A \approx \frac{1}{2}(3.14 \cdot [\quad]^2)$

Substitute 3.14 for π and [ ] for r.

$A \approx \frac{1}{2}([\qquad]) \approx [\qquad]$

Multiply.

Step 3: Add the areas to find the total area.

$A \approx [\qquad] + [\qquad] = $ [ ]

The area of the irregular figure is about [ ] m^2.

© Houghton Mifflin Harcourt Publishing Company

Holt McDougal Mathematics

LESSON 3

Measurement and Geometry

Area of Irregular Figures, *continued*

Example 3 PROBLEM SOLVING APPLICATION

The Wrights want to tile their entry with square foot tiles. How much tile will they need?

5 ft
8 ft
4 ft
7 ft

1. **Understand the Problem**

   Rewrite the question as a statement.

   • Find the amount of tile needed to cover the entry.

   List the important information:

   • The entry is a composite figure.

   • The amount of tile needed is equal to the [ ] of the entry.

2. **Make a Plan**

   Find the area of the entry by separating the figure into familiar figures:

   a [   ] and a [   ]. Then add the areas
   of the rectangle and trapezoid to find the total area.

3. **Solve**

   Find the area of each smaller figure.

   Area of the rectangle: Area of the trapezoid:

   $A = lw$ $A = \frac{1}{2}h(b^1 + b^2)$

   $A = \boxed{} \cdot \boxed{}$ $A = \frac{1}{2} \cdot \boxed{} \, (\boxed{} + \boxed{})$

   $A = \boxed{}$ $A = \frac{1}{2} \cdot 4(\boxed{}) = \boxed{}$

   Add the areas to find the total area.

   $A = \boxed{} + \boxed{} = \boxed{}$

   The Wrights need $\boxed{}$ ft^2 of tile.

4. **Look Back**

   The area of the entry must be greater than the area of the rectangle
   (40 ft^2), so the answer is reasonable.

© Houghton Mifflin Harcourt Publishing Company

Holt McDougal Mathematics

Measurement and Geometry
Area of Irregular Figures, continued

Check It Out!

1. Estimate the shaded area. Each square represents one square foot.

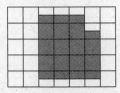

2. Find the area of the figure.

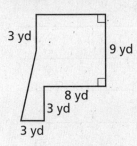

3. The Franklins want to wallpaper the wall of their daughter's loft. How much wallpaper will they need?

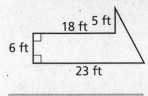

© Houghton Mifflin Harcourt Publishing Company

Measurement and Geometry
Introduction to Three-Dimensional Figures

Lesson Objectives

Identify various three-dimensional figures

Vocabulary

face _____

_____

edge _____

_____

polyhedron _____

_____

vertex _____

_____

base _____

_____

prism _____

_____

pyramid _____

_____

cylinder _____

_____

cone _____

_____

sphere _____

_____

© Houghton Mifflin Harcourt Publishing Company

Holt McDougal Mathematics

Measurement and Geometry

Introduction to Three-Dimensional Figures, continued

Additional Examples

Example 1

Identify the bases and faces of each figure. Then name the figure.

A.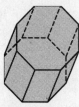

There are two bases, and they are both [   ].

The other faces are [   ].

The figure is an [   ].

Example 2

Classify each figure as a polyhedron or not a polyhedron. Then name the figure.

A.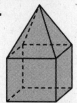

The figure [   ] a polyhedron.

The figure is made up of a rectangular [   ] and

a rectangular [   ].

Check It Out!

1. Identify the bases and faces of the figure. Then name the figure.

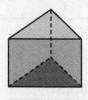

© Houghton Mifflin Harcourt Publishing Company

Measurement and Geometry
Volume of Prisms and Cylinders

Lesson Objectives

Find the volume of prisms and cylinders

Vocabulary

volume _____

_____

Additional Examples

Example 1

Find the volume of each figure.

A. 4 ft, 4 ft, 12 ft

$V = Bh$ Use the formula.

The bases are [   ].

The area of each rectangular

base is [   ] $\cdot$ [   ] $=$ [   ].

$V = 48 \cdot$ [   ]   Substitute for B and h.

$V =$ [   ]   Multiply.

The volume to the nearest tenth is [   ] ft³.

Example 2

A can of tuna is shaped like a cylinder. Find its volume to the nearest tenth. Use 3.14 for π.

$V = \pi r^2 h$ Use the formula.

5 cm

4.2 cm

The radius of the cylinder is [   ] cm,

and the height is [   ] cm.

$V \approx 3.14 \cdot$ [   ]² $\cdot 4.2$ Substitute for r and h.

$V \approx$ [   ]   Multiply.

The volume is about cm³.

© Houghton Mifflin Harcourt Publishing Company

Measurement and Geometry

Volume of Prisms and Cylinders, continued

Example 3

Find the volume of the composite figure.

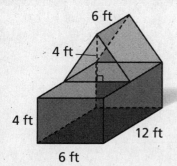

volume of composite figure	=	volume of rectangular prism	+	volume of triangular prism

$$V = \boxed{} + Bh$$

$$V = (\boxed{} \cdot \boxed{})(\boxed{}) + (\boxed{} \cdot \boxed{} \cdot \boxed{})(\boxed{})$$

$$V = \boxed{} + \boxed{}$$

$$V = \boxed{}$$

The volume of the composite figure is ▢ .

Check It Out!

1. Find the volume of the prism to the nearest tenth.

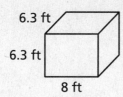

2. Find the volume of the cylinder to the nearest tenth. Use 3.14 for π.

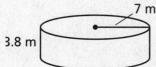

Holt McDougal Mathematics

© Houghton Mifflin Harcourt Publishing Company

Measurement and Geometry
Surface Area of Prisms and Cylinders

Lesson Objectives

Find the surface area of prisms and cylinders

Vocabulary

net _____

_____

surface area _____

_____

lateral face _____

_____

lateral area _____

_____

Additional Examples

Example 1

Find the surface area of the prism.

9 in.   15 in.   7 in.

$S = 2B + Ph$ Use the formula.

$S = 2\left(\boxed{}\right)\left(\boxed{}\right) + \left(\boxed{}\right)\left(\boxed{}\right)$ Substitute P = 2(7) + 2(15) =

$\boxed{} + \boxed{} = \boxed{}$.

$S = \boxed{} + \boxed{}$ Multiply.

$S = \boxed{}$ Add.

The surface area of the prism is $\boxed{}$ in².

© Houghton Mifflin Harcourt Publishing Company

Measurement and Geometry
Surface Area of Prisms and Cylinders, continued

Example 2

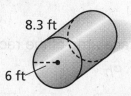
8.3 ft
6 ft

Find the surface area of the cylinder to the nearest tenth. Use 3.14 for π.

$S = 2\pi r^2 + 2\pi rh$ Use the formula.

$S \approx (2 \cdot \boxed{} \cdot \boxed{}^2) +$

$\qquad (2 \cdot \boxed{} \cdot \boxed{} \cdot \boxed{} \cdot \pi)$ Substitute.

$S \approx \boxed{} + \boxed{}$ Multiply.

$S \approx \boxed{}$ Add.

$S \approx \boxed{}$ Round.

The surface area of the cylinder is about ft^2.

Example 3   PROBLEM SOLVING APPLICATION

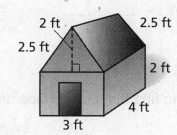
2 ft   2.5 ft
2.5 ft
2 ft
4 ft
3 ft

The playhouse is a composite figure with a floor and no windows. What is the surface area of the playhouse?

1. Understand the Problem

The playhouse is a $\boxed{}$ prism and a $\boxed{}$ prism.

The base of the playhouse is $\boxed{}$ ft by $\boxed{}$ ft and the height is $\boxed{}$ ft.

The base of the roof is $\boxed{}$ ft by $\boxed{}$ ft and the height is $\boxed{}$ ft.

2. Make a Plan

Draw the nets of the figures and shade the parts that show the surface area of the playhouse.

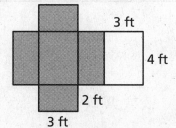
3 ft
4 ft
2 ft
3 ft

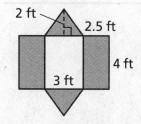
2 ft
2.5 ft
4 ft
3 ft

© Houghton Mifflin Harcourt Publishing Company

3. Solve

Find the surface area of the rectangular prism.

$S = B + Ph$

$= (\boxed{})(\boxed{}) + (\boxed{})(\boxed{})$ Use only $\boxed{}$ base.

$= \boxed{} + \boxed{}$

$= \boxed{}$

Find the surface area of the triangular prism.

$S = 2B + Ph - lw$ $\boxed{}$ the area of the bottom of the triangular prism.

$S = 2(\frac{1}{2}bh) + Ph - lw$

$= 2(\frac{1}{2})(\boxed{})(\boxed{}) + (\boxed{})(\boxed{}) - (\boxed{})(\boxed{})$

$= \boxed{} + \boxed{} - \boxed{}$

$= \boxed{}$

Add to find the total surface area: $\boxed{} + \boxed{} = \boxed{}$.

The surface area of the playhouse is $\boxed{}$.

4. Look Back

The surface area of the playhouse should be less than the surface area of a rectangular prism with the same base and a height of 4 ft.

$S = 2B + Ph = 2(\boxed{})(\boxed{}) + (\boxed{})(\boxed{}) = \boxed{}$

$\boxed{}$ ft^2 is less than $\boxed{}$ ft^2, so the answer is reasonable.

© Houghton Mifflin Harcourt Publishing Company

Measurement and Geometry

Surface Area of Prisms and Cylinders, continued

Check It Out!

1. Find the surface area of the prism.

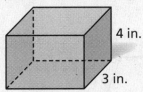

4 in.

3 in.

6 in.

2. Find the surface area of the cylinder to the nearest tenth. Use 3.14 for π.

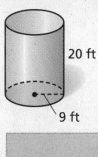

20 ft

9 ft

© Houghton Mifflin Harcourt Publishing Company

Holt McDougal Mathematics

Measurement and Geometry
Chapter Review

Know it!
Note

1 Perimeter and Circumference

Find the perimeter of each polygon.

1.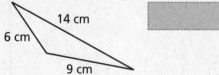
14 cm
6 cm
9 cm

2.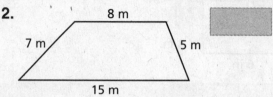
8 m
7 m
5 m
15 m

2 Area of Circles

Find the area of each circle to the nearest tenth. Use 3.14 for π.

3.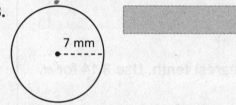
7 mm

4.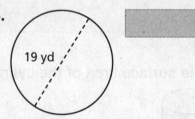
19 yd

3 Area of Irregular Figures

Find the area of each figure. Use 3.14 for π.

5.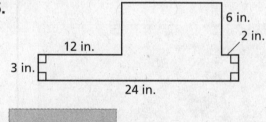
6 in.
2 in.
12 in.
3 in.
24 in.

6.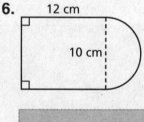
12 cm
10 cm

4 Introduction to Three-Dimensional Figures

Classify each figure as a polyhedron or not a polyhedron. Then name the figure.

7.

8.

9.

© Houghton Mifflin Harcourt Publishing Company

Holt McDougal Mathematics

Measurement and Geometry
Chapter Review, continued

5 Volume of Prisms and Cylinders

Find the volume of each figure to the nearest tenth. Use 3.14 for π.

10.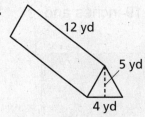
12 yd
5 yd
4 yd

11.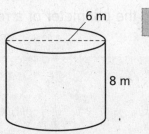
6 m
8 m

12. A shipping box is shaped like a rectangular prism. It is 12 in. long, 7 in. wide, and 4 in. high. Find its volume.

13. A can of bubbles is shaped like a cylinder. It is 5 cm wide and 13 cm tall. Find its volume to the nearest tenth. Use 3.14 for π.

6 Surface Area of Prisms and Cylinders

Find the surface area of the prism formed by the net.

14.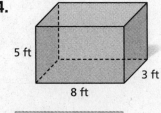
5 ft
3 ft
8 ft

15.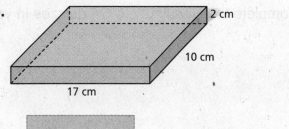
2 cm
10 cm
17 cm

16. A can of play dough is cylindrical. The can is 7 cm wide and 7 cm tall. If the label on the can is 3 cm tall and goes all around the can, how much paper is needed for the label to the nearest tenth? Use 3.14 for π.

© Houghton Mifflin Harcourt Publishing Company

Measurement and Geometry

Big Ideas

Answer these questions to summarize the important concepts from Chapter 9 in your own words.

1. Explain how to find the perimeter of a rectangle with length 19 inches and width 14 inches.

2. Explain how to find the area of a circle with diameter 16 yards.

For more review to Chapter 9:

- Complete the Chapter 9 Study Guide and Review in your textbook.
- Complete the Ready to Go On quizzes in your textbook.

© Houghton Mifflin Harcourt Publishing Company

Holt McDougal Mathematics

Lesson Objectives

Use informal measures of probability

Vocabulary

experiment _____

trial _____

outcome _____

event _____

probability _____

complement _____

simple event _____

compound event _____

Additional Examples

Example 1

Determine whether each event is impossible, unlikely, as likely as not, likely, or certain.

A. rolling an odd number on a number cube
There are 6 possible outcomes:

Odd	*Not* Odd
1, 3, 5	2, 4, 6

[____] of the outcomes are odd.

Rolling an odd number is [_____]

© Houghton Mifflin Harcourt Publishing Company

Probability
Probability, continued

Example 2

A bag contains circular chips that are the same size and weight. There are 8 purple, 4 pink, 8 white, and 2 blue chips in the bag. The probability of drawing a pink chip is $\frac{2}{11}$. What is the probability of not drawing a pink chip?

$P(\text{event}) + P(\text{complement}) = \boxed{}$

$P(\text{pink}) + P(\text{not pink}) = \boxed{}$

$\boxed{} + P(\text{not pink}) = \boxed{}$ Substitute $\boxed{}$ for $P(\text{pink})$.

$\dfrac{-\boxed{} \qquad\qquad -\boxed{}}{}$ Subtract $\boxed{}$ from both sides.

$P(\text{not pink}) = \boxed{}$

The probability of not drawing a pink marble is $\boxed{}$.

Example 3

Mandy's science teacher almost always introduces a new chapter by conducting an experiment. Mandy's class finished a chapter on Friday. Should Mandy expect the teacher to conduct an experiment next week? Explain.

Since the class just finished a chapter, they will be starting a new chapter.

It is $\boxed{}$ the teacher will conduct an experiment.

Check It Out!

1. Determine whether the event is impossible, unlikely, as likely as not, or certain.

rolling a 2 or 4 on a number cube

$\boxed{}$

© Houghton Mifflin Harcourt Publishing Company

   Holt McDougal Mathematics

Probability

Experimental Probability

Lesson Objectives

Find experimental probability

Vocabulary

experimental probability _____

_____

Additional Examples

Example 1

During skating practice, Sasha landed 7 out of 12 jumps. What is the experimental probability that she will land her next jump?

$$P \approx \frac{\text{number of times an event occurs}}{\text{total number of trails}}$$

$$P(\text{land}) \approx \frac{\text{number of jumps} \quad \boxed{}}{\text{number of jumps} \quad \boxed{}}$$

$$\approx \boxed{} \qquad \text{Substitute.}$$

The experimental probability that Sasha will land her next jump is $\boxed{}$.

Example 2

Students have checked out 55 books from the library. Of these, 32 books are fiction.

A. What is the experimental probability that the next book checked out will be fiction?

$$P(\text{fiction}) \approx \frac{\text{number of} \quad \boxed{} \quad \text{books checked out}}{\text{total number of books checked out}}$$

$$\approx \boxed{} \qquad \text{Substitute.}$$

The experimental probability that the next book checked out will be fiction

is approximately $\boxed{}$.

© Houghton Mifflin Harcourt Publishing Company

Holt McDougal Mathematics

Probability

Experimental Probability, continued

Students have checked out 55 books from the library. Of these, 32 books are fiction.

B. What is the experimental probability that the next book checked out will be nonfiction?

$P(\text{nonfiction}) \approx \dfrac{\text{number of } \boxed{} \text{ books checked out}}{\text{total number of books checked out}}$

$\approx \boxed{}$ Substitute.

The experimental probability that the next book checked out will be nonfiction

is approximately $\boxed{}$.

Check It Out!

1. During basketball practice, Martha made 9 out of 10 free throws. What is the experimental probability that she will make her next attempt?

2. Students have a fruit choice for lunch of an apple or a pear. So far 18 of 47 students have selected pears. What is the experimental probability that the next fruit selected will be an apple?

© Houghton Mifflin Harcourt Publishing Company

Holt McDougal Mathematics

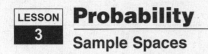

LESSON 3 Probability

Sample Spaces

Know it! Note

Lesson Objectives

Use counting methods to determine possible outcomes

Vocabulary

sample space _____

_____

Fundamental Counting Principle _____

_____

_____

Additional Examples

Example 1 PROBLEM SOLVING APPLICATION

One bag has a red tile, a blue tile, and a green tile. A second bag has a red tile and a blue tile. Vincent draws one tile from each bag. What are all the possible outcomes? How many outcomes are in the sample space?

1. Understand the Problem

Rewrite the question as a statement.

- Find all the possible [ ] of drawing one tile from each

  bag, and determine the size of the [ ] space.

List the important information:

- There are [ ] bags.

- One bag has a [ ] tile, a [ ] tile, and a [ ] tile.

- The other bag has a [ ] tile and a [ ] tile.

© Houghton Mifflin Harcourt Publishing Company

Holt McDougal Mathematics

Probability

Sample Spaces, continued

2. **Make a Plan**

You can make an organized list to show all possible outcomes.

3. **Solve**

Let R = red tile, B = blue tile, and G = green tile.
Record each possible outcome.

The possible outcomes are

[ ] , [ ] , [ ] , [ ] , [ ] ,

and [ ] . There are [ ] possible
outcomes in the sample space.

4. **Look Back**

Each possible outcome that is recorded in the list is different.

Bag 1	Bag 2

Example 2

There are 4 cards and 2 tiles in a board game. The cards are labeled N, S,
E, and W. The tiles are numbered 1 and 2. A player randomly selects one
card and one tile. What are all the possible outcomes? How many
outcomes are in the sample space?

You can make a [ ] diagram to show the sample space.

List each letter of the cards. Then list each color of the tiles.

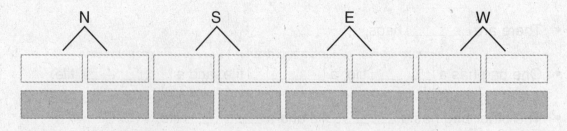

There are [ ] possible outcomes in the sample space.

© Houghton Mifflin Harcourt Publishing Company

Holt McDougal Mathematics

Probability

Sample Spaces, continued

Example 3

Carrie rolls two 1-6 number cubes. How many outcomes are possible?

The first number cube has ☐ outcomes.

The second number cube has ☐ outcomes.

☐ · ☐ = ▢   Use the Fundamental Counting Principle.

There are ▢ possible outcomes.

Check It Out!

1. Darren has two bags of marbles. One has a green marble and a red marble. The second bag has a blue and a red marble. Darren draws one marble from each bag. What are all the possible outcomes? How many outcomes are in the sample space?

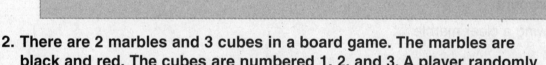

2. There are 2 marbles and 3 cubes in a board game. The marbles are black and red. The cubes are numbered 1, 2, and 3. A player randomly selects one marble and one cube. What are all the possible outcomes? How many outcomes are in the sample space?

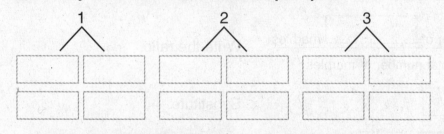

3. Juan tosses a coin and rolls a number cube. How many outcomes are possible?

© Houghton Mifflin Harcourt Publishing Company

Probability
Theoretical Probability

Know it!
Note

Lesson Objectives

Find the theoretical probability of an event

Vocabulary

theoretical probability _____

_____

equally likely _____

_____

fair _____

Additional Examples

Example 1

Andy has 20 marbles in a bag. Of these, 9 are clear and 11 are blue. Find the probability of each event. Write your answer as a fraction, a decimal, and a percent.

A. drawing a clear marble

$$P = \frac{\text{number of } \boxed{} \text{ outcomes}}{\text{total number of } \boxed{} \text{ outcomes}}$$

$$P(\text{clear}) = \frac{\text{number of } \boxed{} \text{ marbles}}{\text{total number of marbles}} \qquad \text{Write the ratio.}$$

$$= \boxed{} \qquad\qquad\qquad \text{Substitute.}$$

$$= \boxed{} = \boxed{} \% \qquad \text{Write as a decimal and write as a percent.}$$

The theoretical probability of drawing a clear marble is ▢ , ▢ ,

or ▢ %.

© Houghton Mifflin Harcourt Publishing Company

Holt McDougal Mathematics

Probability

Theoretical Probability, continued

Example 2

There are 13 boys and 10 girls on the track team. The name of each team member is written on an index card. A card is drawn at random to choose a student to run a sprint and the card is replaced in the stack.

A. Find the theoretical probability of drawing a boy's name.

$$P(\text{boy}) = \frac{\text{number of } \boxed{} \text{ on the team}}{\text{number of } \boxed{} \text{ on the team}}$$ Find the theoretical probability.

$$= \boxed{}$$ Substitute.

Check It Out!

1. Find the probability. Write your answer as a fraction, as a decimal, and as a percent. Jane has 20 marbles in a bag. Of these 8 are green. Find the probability of drawing a green marble from the bag.

2. There are 15 boys and 12 girls in the class. Find the theoretical probability of drawing a boy's name.

© Houghton Mifflin Harcourt Publishing Company

Holt McDougal Mathematics

Probability

Making Predictions

Lesson Objectives

Use probability to predict events.

Vocabulary

prediction _____

_____

Additional Examples

Example 1

Lawrence finds that his experimental probability of getting a hit is 40%. Out of 350 at-bats, how many times can he expect to get a hit?

Method 1: Set up an equation.

$\boxed{} \cdot \boxed{} = x$ Multiply the probability by the total number of $\boxed{}$.

$\boxed{} = x$ Solve for x.

Method 2: Set up a proportion.

$\dfrac{4}{10} = \boxed{}$ Think: 4 out of 10 is how many out of $\boxed{}$?

$\boxed{} \cdot \boxed{} = \boxed{} \cdot \boxed{}$ The cross products are equal.

$\boxed{} = 10x$ Multiply.

$\dfrac{1,400}{10} = \dfrac{10x}{10}$ Divide each side by $\boxed{}$ to isolate the variable.

$\boxed{} = x$

Lawrence can expect to get a hit times.

Probability
Making Predictions, continued

Example 2

A spinner has eight sections of equal size. Three sections are labeled 1, two are labeled 2, and the others are labeled 3, 4, and 5. In 50 spins, how often can you expect to spin a 1?

$P(1) = \dfrac{3}{8}$

$\dfrac{3}{8} = \boxed{}$ Think: 3 out of 8 is how many

out of $\boxed{}$?

$\boxed{} \cdot \boxed{} = \boxed{} \cdot \boxed{}$ The cross products are equal.

$\boxed{} = 8x$ Multiply.

$\dfrac{150}{8} = \dfrac{8x}{8}$ Divide each side by $\boxed{}$ to isolate the variable.

$\boxed{} = x$

You can expect the spinner to land on a 1 about $\boxed{}$ times.

Example 3   PROBLEM SOLVING APPLICATION

The Singh family is planning a 7-day tropical vacation during July or August. The island destination they have chosen averages 21 rainy days during this 62-day period. If the Singhs would like to avoid rain on at least 5 days of their vacation, should they go to this spot or choose another?

1. Understand the Problem

The answer will be whether the Singhs should go to the tropical island.

List the important information:

The Singhs are planning a $\boxed{}$-day vacation.

The island destination averages $\boxed{}$ rainy days during this $\boxed{}$-day period.

The Singhs would like to avoid rain on at least $\boxed{}$ days of their vacation.

2. Make a Plan

On average $\boxed{}$ out of $\boxed{}$ days are rainy. After finding out the number of rainy days there should be for 7 days, subtract to find the number of non- rainy days.

© Houghton Mifflin Harcourt Publishing Company

      Holt McDougal Mathematics

3. Solve

$\dfrac{21}{62} = $ [ ]

Think: 21 out of 62 is how many out of [ ]?

[ ] · [ ] = [ ] · [ ]

The cross products are equal.

[ ] = 62x

Multiply.

$\dfrac{147}{62} = \dfrac{62x}{62}$

Divide each side by [ ] to isolate the variable to find the number of rainy days.

[ ] ≈ x

There will be about [ ] or [ ] rainy days in 7 days.

[ ] the predicted number of rainy days from the total vacation days.

7 − 3 = [ ]

The Singhs should choose [ ] location.

4. Look Back

It is likely to rain more than [ ] days (about [ ] days) during a 7-day

period, which [ ] give the Singhs at least 5 sunny days.

Check It Out!

1. **Marty finds the experimental probability of him making a field goal to be 74%. Out of 150 field goal attempts, how many times can he expect to make a field goal?**

2. **Rhonda rolls a number cube 330 times. How many times can she expect to roll a 5?**

3. **The Berry family is planning a 12-day vacation to a beach. The beach they have chosen averages 45 rainy days during this 109-day period. If the Berrys would like to avoid rain on at least 7 days of their vacation, should they go to this spot or choose another?**

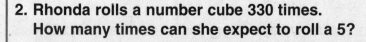

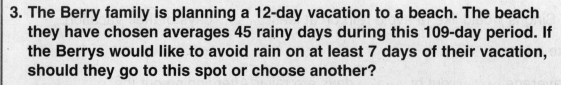

© Houghton Mifflin Harcourt Publishing Company

Holt McDougal Mathematics

LESSON 6 Probability

Probability of Independent and Dependent Events

Lesson Objectives

Find the probability of independent and dependent events

Vocabulary

independent events _____

_____

dependent events _____

_____

Additional Examples

Example 1

Decide whether each set of events are dependent or independent. Explain your answer.

A. Kathi draws a 4 from a set of cards numbered 1–10 and rolls a 2 on a number cube.

Since the outcome of drawing the card does not [   ] the

outcome of rolling the cube, the events are [   ].

Example 2

Find the probability of choosing a green marble at random from a bag containing 5 green and 10 white marbles and then flipping a coin and getting tails.

The outcome of choosing the marble does not [   ] the

outcome of flipping the coin, so the events are [   ].

$P(\text{green and tails}) = P(\text{green}) \cdot P(\text{tails}) = $ [   ] $\cdot$ [   ]

The probability of choosing a green marble and a coin landing on tails

is [   ].

© Houghton Mifflin Harcourt Publishing Company

171   **Holt McDougal Mathematics**

Probability

Probability of Independent and Dependent Events, continued

Example 3

A reading list contains 5 historical books and 3 science-fiction books.
What is the probability that Juan will randomly choose a historical book
for his first report and a science-fiction book for his second?

The first choice changes the number of books left, and may change the

number of science-fiction books left, so the events are [   ].

P(historical) = [   ]   There are [ ] historical books out

of [ ] books.

P(science-fiction) = [   ]   There are [ ] science-fiction books

left out of [ ] books.

P(historical and then science-fiction) = $P(A) \cdot P(B \text{ after } A)$

= [ ] · [ ]   Multiply.

The probability of Juan choosing a historical book and then choosing a

science-fiction book is [   ].

Check It Out!

1. Decide whether the set of events are dependent or independent.
   Explain your answer. Annabelle chooses a blue marble from a set of
   three, each of different colors, and then Louise chooses a second
   marble from the remaining two marbles.

2. Find the probability of choosing a red marble at random from a bag
   containing 5 red and 5 white marbles and then flipping a coin and
   getting heads.

© Houghton Mifflin Harcourt Publishing Company

Holt McDougal Mathematics

Probability

Combinations

Lesson Objectives

Find the number of possible combinations

Vocabulary

combination _____

_____

Additional Examples

Example 1

Kristy's Diner offers customers a choice of 4 side dishes with each order: carrots, corn, french fries, and mashed potatoes. How many different combinations of 3 side dishes can Kareem choose?

Begin by listing all the [_____] choices of side dishes taken three at a time.

Because [_____] does not matter, you can eliminate repeated triples. For example 1, 2, 3 is already listed, so 2, 1, 3 can be eliminated.

1, 2, 3	2, 1, 3	3, 1, 2	4, 1, 2
1, 2, 4	2, 1, 4	3, 1, 4	4, 1, 3
1, 3, 4	2, 3, 4	3, 2, 4	4, 2, 3

There are [____] possible combinations of 3 side dishes Kareem can choose with his order.

© Houghton Mifflin Harcourt Publishing Company

Holt McDougal Mathematics

Probability

Combinations, continued

Example 2 **PROBLEM SOLVING APPLICATION**

Lara is going to make a double-dip cone from a choice of vanilla, chocolate, and strawberry. She wants each dip to be a different flavor. How many different cone combinations can she choose?

1. Understand the Problem
Rewrite the question as a statement.

- Find the number of possible [   ] of two flavors Lara can choose.

List the important information:

- There are [   ] flavor choices in all.

2. Make a Plan

You can make a [   ] diagram to show the possible combinations.

3. Solve

The tree diagram shows [   ] possible ways, but each combination is listed twice. So there are [   ] ÷ [   ] = [   ] possible combinations.

4. Look Back
You can also check by making a list. The vanilla can be paired with two other flavors and the chocolate with one. The total number of possible pairs is 2 + 1 = 3.

Check It Out!

1. Jim has 4 shirts of different colors: red, green, blue, and yellow (r, g, b, y). He plans to pack 3 of them. How many different combinations of 3 shirts can Jim choose?

Holt McDougal Mathematics

© Houghton Mifflin Harcourt Publishing Company

Probability
Permutations

Lesson Objectives

Find the number of possible permutations

Vocabulary

permutation _____

_____

factorial _____

_____

Additional Examples

Example 1

In how many different orders can you arrange the letters _A_, _B_, and _T_?

Use a list to find the possible _____ .

There are [ ] ways to order the letters.

Holt McDougal Mathematics

© Houghton Mifflin Harcourt Publishing Company

Probability

Permutations, continued

Example 2

Mary, Rob, Carla, and Eli are lining up for lunch. In how many different ways can they line up for lunch?

Once you fill a position, you have one less choice for the next position.

There are ☐ choices for the first position.

There are ☐ remaining choices for the second position.

There are ☐ remaining choices for the third position.

There is ☐ choice left for the fourth position.

☐ · ☐ · ☐ · ☐ = ☐ Multiply.

There are ☐ different ways the students can line up for lunch.

Example 3

How many different orders are possible for Shellie to line up 8 books on a shelf?

Number of permutations = 8!

= ☐ · ☐ · ☐ · ☐ · ☐ · ☐ · ☐ · ☐

= ☐

There are ☐ different ways for Shellie to line up 8 books on the shelf.

Check It Out!

1. In how many ways can you arrange the colors red, orange, blue?

☐

© Houghton Mifflin Harcourt Publishing Company

Probability
Probability of Compound Events

Lesson Objective

Learn to find probabilities of compound events using organized lists, tables, or tree diagrams.

Additional Examples

Example 1

A pizza parlor offers seven different pizza toppings: pineapple, mushrooms, Canadian bacon, onions, pepperoni, beef, and sausage. What is the probability that a random order for a two-topping pizza includes pepperoni?

Let Pi = Pineapple, M = mushrooms, C = Canadian bacon, O = onions, Pe = pepperoni, B = beef, S = sausage.

Pi-M	M-C	☐	O-Pe
Pi-C	☐	C-Pe	☐
Pi-O	M-Pe	C-B	O-S
☐	M-B	C-S	O̶-̶P̶i̶
Pi-B	M-S	C̶-̶P̶i̶	O̶-̶M̶
Pi-S		C̶-̶M̶	O̶-̶C̶

Pe-B	☐	S̶-̶P̶i̶
☐	B̶-̶P̶i̶	S̶-̶M̶
P̶e̶-̶P̶i̶	B̶-̶M̶	S̶-̶C̶
P̶e̶-̶M̶	B̶-̶C̶	S̶-̶O̶
P̶e̶-̶C̶	B̶-̶O̶	S̶-̶P̶e̶
P̶e̶-̶O̶	B̶-̶P̶e̶	S̶-̶B̶

List all the possible two-topping pizzas.

Because the order of the toppings does not matter, you can eliminate repeated pairs.

There are ☐ equally likely two-topping pizzas.

There are ☐ equally likely two-topping pizzas.

There are ☐ pizzas that include pepperoni.

$$P(\text{Pe}) = \frac{\text{number of pizzas with pepperoni}}{\text{total number of equally likely two-topping pizzas}} = \frac{☐}{☐}$$

The probability that a random two-topping pizza order will include pepperoni is ☐ .

Holt McDougal Mathematics

© Houghton Mifflin Harcourt Publishing Company

Probability

Probability of Compound Events, continued

LESSON
Probability
Probability of Comp

Example 2

Jack, Kate, and Linda line up in random order in the cafeteria. What is the probability that Kate randomly lines up between Jack and Linda?

☐ K—L → ☐   List permutations
  L—K → ☐   beginning with Jack.

☐ J—L → ☐   List permutations
  L—J → ☐   beginning with Kate.

☐ J—K → ☐   List permutations
  K—J → ☐   beginning with Linda.

P(Kate in middle) = $\dfrac{\text{number of line-ups with Kate in middle}}{\text{total number of equally likely line-ups}}$ = ☐ = ☐

The probability that Kate randomly lines up between Jack and Linda is ☐.

Example 3

Mika rolls 2 number cubes. What is the probability that the sum of the two numbers will be less than 4?

Make a table of possible outcomes in the sample ☐.

Circle all the pairs of numbers that have a sum less than ☐.

	1	2	3	4	5	6
1	1-1	1-2	☐	1-4	1-5	1-6
2	2-1	2-2	2-3	☐	2-5	2-6
3	3-1	☐	3-3	3-4	3-5	3-6
4	4-1	4-2	4-3	4-4	4-5	☐
5	☐	5-2	5-3	5-4	5-5	5-6
6	6-1	6-2	6-3	6-4	☐	6-6

There are ☐ out of ☐ possible outcomes that have a sum less than 4.

The probability of rolling a sum less than 4 is ☐ = , or about 8%.

© Houghton Mifflin Harcourt Publishing Company

Probability

Probability of Compound Events, continued

Check It Out!

1. A gallery has 4 paintings, labeled I, II, III, and IV. The gallery manager randomly selects 2 paintings for display in the front window each week. What is the probability she will randomly select I and II the first week?

2. Brian has these 4 letter tiles: I, Q, T, and U. If he randomly positions the tiles, what is the probability that Brian will make a word?

© Houghton Mifflin Harcourt Publishing Company

1 Probability

Determine whether each event is impossible, unlikely, as likely as not, likely, or certain.

1. rolling a 7 on a number cube

2. flipping a coin and getting heads

3. drawing a red marble from a bag with 7 blue marbles and 10 red marbles

4. Charlie rolls two number cubes. The probability the sum is less than 4 is $\frac{2}{21}$. What is the probability of having a sum of 4 or greater?

5. Anna exercises for at least 45 minutes on days she has to work. If it is Monday and Anna has to work, would you expect her to exercise over 30 minutes? Explain.

2 Experimental Probability

6. David made 16 out of 28 free throws at basketball practice. What is the experimental probability of making his next free throw?

7. Christina scored an A on 7 out of 10 math quizzes this quarter. What is the experimental probability that she scores an A on her next math quiz?

8. For the past two weeks, Courtney has picked 9 long sleeve and 6 short sleeve shirts to wear to school.

   a) What is the probability that the next shirt she picks will be short sleeve?

   b) What is the probability that the next shirt she picks will be long sleeve?

Holt McDougal Mathematics

© Houghton Mifflin Harcourt Publishing Company

3 Sample Spaces

9. Chad has blue pants and tan pants. He also has a white shirt, gray shirt, blue shirt and a yellow shirt. What are all the possible outcomes for an outfit? How many outcomes are in the sample space?

10. McKenzie has a sundae bar for her birthday party. It has vanilla, chocolate and strawberry ice cream. For toppings it has hot fudge, caramel sauce, and marshmallow topping. What are all the possible outcomes for a sundae? How many outcomes are in the sample space?

4 Theoretical Probability

A twelve-sided number cube is rolled. What is the probability of each event?

11. P(even number)

12. P(greater than 10)

13. P(less than 6)

14. P(9)

15. Lucy and her cousins are choosing names to buy gifts for each other. She has 6 boy cousins and 7 girl cousins. If Lucy is randomly picking one of her cousin's names, what is the probability she picks a girl?

5 Making Predictions

16. Carrie finds her experimental probability of hitting a homerun to be 14%. Out of 250 at-bats, how many times can she expect to hit a homerun?

Bryan rolled a number cube 24 times.

17. How many times can Bryan expect to roll a 6?

18. How many times can Bryan expect to roll a number less than 4?

© Houghton Mifflin Harcourt Publishing Company

Probability

Chapter Review, continued

6 Probability of Independent and Dependent Events

Decide whether each set of events is independent or dependent. Explain.

19. A man chooses a movie at the video store and then chooses a second movie from those remaining.

20. A child takes a coin out of his piggybank and then picks another one after replacing the first coin.

21. Julio has a bag of marbles that contains 6 red, 11 blue, 5 green, and 10 yellow. What is the probability Julio picks a green marble first and then picks a red marble without replacing the green marble?

7 Combinations

22. Gino's pizza offers 5 toppings, pepperoni, sausage, mushrooms, green peppers, and extra cheese, for their pizzas. How many different 3 topping pizzas can be made?

23. Graham, Lupe, Chandra and Karl are going to play checkers. How many different ways can they pair up?

24. A student takes 2 electives in a year. How many different combinations of 2 electives can be formed from 10 elective choices?

© Houghton Mifflin Harcourt Publishing Company

Holt McDougal Mathematics

8 Permutations

25. A family of 5 is posing for a family picture. If they want to stand in a line, how many different orders can they make?

26. Students in a computer class need to create a 4-digit password using the numbers 1-9 without repeating. How many different passwords can be created?

27. Find the number of permutations of the letters in the word "MATH"?

Determine whether each problem involves combinations or permutations. Explain your answer.

28. Picking 6 people to play a game out of 10 people.

29. The seating order in your math class

9 Probability of Compound Events

30. Mike rolls two number cubes. What is the probability that Mike rolls an even number?

31. Out of 12 choices for sandwiches, beef, chicken, and turkey are the three favorites. If a sandwich is to be made using two of the 12 choices, what is the probability that two of the three favorite choices will be used on the sandwich?

© Houghton Mifflin Harcourt Publishing Company

Holt McDougal Mathematics

Probability
Big Ideas

Answer these questions to summarize the important concepts from Chapter 10 in your own words.

1. Tony answered 27 out of 30 questions correctly. Explain how to find the experimental probability that Tony will answer the next question correctly.

2. Explain how to find the theoretical probability of rolling a number greater than 4 on a fair number cube.

3. Explain the difference between combinations and permutations.

For more review of Chapter 10:

- Complete the Chapter 10 Study Guide and Review in your textbook.
- Complete the Ready to Go On quizzes in your textbook.

© Houghton Mifflin Harcourt Publishing Company

Holt McDougal Mathematics

Multi-Step Equations and Inequalities
Solving Two-Step Equations

Lesson Objectives

Solve two-step equations

Additional Examples

Example 1

Solve.

A. $9c + 3 = 39$

$$-\boxed{} \quad -\boxed{}$$

Subtract $\boxed{}$ from both sides.

$$9c = \boxed{}$$

$$\boxed{} = \boxed{}$$

Divide both sides by $\boxed{}$.

$$c = \boxed{}$$

Example 2

Solve.

A. $\quad 6 + \dfrac{y}{5} = \quad 21$

$$-\boxed{} \qquad -\boxed{}$$

Subtract $\boxed{}$ from both sides.

$$\dfrac{y}{5} = \boxed{}$$

$$(\boxed{}) \dfrac{y}{5} = (\boxed{}) \, 15$$

Multiply both sides by $\boxed{}$.

$$y = \boxed{}$$

© Houghton Mifflin Harcourt Publishing Company

Holt McDougal Mathematics

Multi-Step Equations and Inequalities

Solving Two-Step Equations, continued

Example 3

Jamie rented a canoe while she was on vacation. She paid a flat rental fee of $85.00 plus $7.50 each day. Her total cost was $130.00. For how many days did she rent the canoe?

Let *d* represent the number of days she rented the canoe.

$7.5d + 85 = 130$

$\underline{-\boxed{}} \quad \underline{-\boxed{}}$ Subtract $\boxed{}$ from both sides.

$7.5d = \boxed{}$

$\boxed{} = \boxed{}$ Divide both sides by $\boxed{}$.

$d = \boxed{}$

Jamie rented the canoe for $\boxed{}$ days.

Check It Out!

1. Solve.

$-6m - 8 = -50$

2. Solve.

$8 + \dfrac{y}{2} = 48$

3. Jack's father rented a car while they were on vacation. He paid a rental fee of $20.00 per day plus 20¢ a mile. He paid $25.00 for mileage and his total bill for renting the car was $165.00. For how many days did he rent the car?

© Houghton Mifflin Harcourt Publishing Company

Holt McDougal Mathematics

LESSON 2 — **Multi-Step Equations and Inequalities**
Solving Multi-Step Equations

Lesson Objectives

Solve multi-step equations

Additional Examples

Example 1

Solve $12 - 7b + 10b = 18$.

$$12 - 7b + 10b = 18$$

$12 + \boxed{}b = 18$ Combine $\boxed{}$ terms.

$-\boxed{} \qquad -\boxed{}$ Subtract $\boxed{}$ from both sides.

$3b = \boxed{}$

$\boxed{} = \boxed{}$ Divide both sides by $\boxed{}$.

$b = \boxed{}$

Example 2

Solve $5(y - 2) + 6 = 21$.

$$5(y - 2) + 6 = 21$$

$5(\boxed{}) - 5(\boxed{}) + 6 = 21$ Distribute $\boxed{}$ on the left side.

$5y - \boxed{} = 21$ Simplify.

$+\boxed{} \qquad +\boxed{}$ Add $\boxed{}$ to both sides.

$5y = \boxed{}$

$\dfrac{5y}{\boxed{}} = \dfrac{25}{\boxed{}}$ Divide both sides by $\boxed{}$.

$y = \boxed{}$

© Houghton Mifflin Harcourt Publishing Company

187   **Holt McDougal Mathematics**

Multi-Step Equations and Inequalities

Solving Multi-Step Equations, continued

Example 3
PROBLEM SOLVING APPLICATION

Troy has three times as many trading cards as Hillary. Subtracting 9 from the number of trading cards Troy has and then dividing by 6 gives the number of cards Sean has. If Sean has 24 trading cards, how many trading cards does Hillary own?

1. Understand the Problem

Rewrite the question as a statement.

- Find the number of trading cards that [   ] has.

List the important information:

- Troy has [   ] times as many trading cards as Hillary has.

- Subtracting 9 from the number of trading cards that [   ] has and then dividing by 6 gives the number of cards [   ] has.

- Sean has [   ] trading cards.

2. Make a Plan

Let c represent the number of trading cards Hillary has. Then $3c$ represents

the number [   ] has, and $\frac{3c-9}{6}$ represents the number [   ]

has, which equals [   ].

Solve the equation $\frac{3c-9}{6} = 24$ for c to find the number of cards

[   ] has.

Holt McDougal Mathematics

© Houghton Mifflin Harcourt Publishing Company

Multi-Step Equations and Inequalities

Solving Multi-Step Equations, continued

3. Solve

$$\frac{3c - 9}{6} = 24$$

$$\left(\boxed{}\right)\frac{3c - 9}{6} = \left(\boxed{}\right)24 \qquad \text{Multiply both sides by } \boxed{}.$$

$$3c - 9 = \boxed{}$$

$$3c - 9 + \boxed{} = 144 + \boxed{} \qquad \text{Add } \boxed{} \text{ to both sides.}$$

$$3c = \boxed{}$$

$$\boxed{} = \boxed{} \qquad \text{Divide both sides by } \boxed{}.$$

$$c = \boxed{}$$

Hillary has ▮▮▮▮ cards.

4. Look Back

If Hillary has $\boxed{}$ cards, then Troy has $\boxed{}$ cards. When you

subtract 9 from 153, you get $\boxed{}$. And 144 divided by 6 is $\boxed{}$,

which is the number of cards that $\boxed{}$ has. So the answer is correct.

Check It Out!

1. Solve $14 - 8b + 12b = 62$.

▮▮▮▮▮▮▮▮▮▮▮▮▮▮▮▮▮▮▮▮▮▮

2. Solve $4(y + 3) - 12 = 116$.

▮▮▮▮▮▮▮▮▮▮▮▮▮▮▮▮▮▮▮▮▮▮

3. John is twice as old as Helen. Subtracting 4 from John's age and then dividing by 2 gives William's age. If William is 24, how old is Helen?

▮▮▮▮▮▮▮▮▮▮▮▮▮▮▮▮▮▮▮▮▮▮

© Houghton Mifflin Harcourt Publishing Company

Multi-Step Equations and Inequalities
Solving Equations with Variables on Both Sides

Lesson Objectives

Solve equations that have variables on both sides

Additional Examples

Example 1

Group the terms with variables on one side of the equal sign, and simplify.

A. $60 - 4y = 8y$

$60 - 4y + \boxed{} = 8y + \boxed{}$ Add $\boxed{}$ to both sides.

$\boxed{} = \boxed{}$ Simplify.

B. $-5b + 72 = -2b$

$-5b + \boxed{} + 72 = -2b + \boxed{}$ Add $\boxed{}$ to both sides.

$\boxed{} = \boxed{}$ Simplify.

Example 2

Solve.

A. $7c = 2c + 55$

$7c - \boxed{} = 2c - \boxed{} + 55$ Subtract $\boxed{}$ from both sides.

$\boxed{} = \boxed{}$ Simplify.

$\boxed{} = \boxed{}$ Divide both sides by $\boxed{}$.

$c = \boxed{}$

© Houghton Mifflin Harcourt Publishing Company

Holt McDougal Mathematics

Multi-Step Equations and Inequalities

Solving Equations with Variables on Both Sides, continued

Example 3

Christine can buy a new snowboard for $136.50. She will still need to rent boots for $8.50 a day. She can rent a snowboard and boots for $18.25 a day. How many days would Christine need to rent both the snowboard and the boots to pay as much as she would if she buys the snowboard and rents only the boots for the season?

Let d represent the number of days.

$$18.25d = 136.5 + 8.5d$$

$18.25d - \boxed{} = 136.5 + 8.5d - \boxed{}$ Subtract $\boxed{}$ from both sides.

$\boxed{}d = \boxed{}$ Simplify.

$\dfrac{9.75d}{\boxed{}} = \dfrac{136.5}{\boxed{}}$ Divide both sides by $\boxed{}$.

$d = \boxed{}$

Christine would need to rent both the snowboard and the boots for

▊▊▊ days to pay as much as she would have if she had bought the snowboard and rented only the boots.

Check It Out!

1. Group the terms with variables on one side of the equal sign, and simplify.

$$-8b + 24 = -5b$$

2. Solve.

$$54 - 3q = 6q + 9$$

3. A local telephone company charges $40 per month for services plus a fee of $0.10 a minute for long distance calls. Another company charges $75.00 a month for unlimited service. How many minutes does it take for a person who subscribes to the first plan to pay as much as a person who subscribes to the unlimited plan?

© Houghton Mifflin Harcourt Publishing Company

Holt McDougal Mathematics

Multi-Step Equations and Inequalities
Inequalities

Lesson Objectives

Read and write inequalities and graph them on a number line

Vocabulary

inequality _____

_____

algebraic inequality _____

_____

solution set _____

_____

compound inequality _____

_____

Additional Examples

Example 1

Write an inequality for each situation.

A. There are at least 15 people in the waiting room.

[gray box]   "At least" means

[box] than or

[box] to.

B. The tram attendant will allow no more than 60 people on the tram.

[gray box]   "No more than" means

[box] than or

[box] to.

© Houghton Mifflin Harcourt Publishing Company

Multi-Step Equations and Inequalities

Inequalities, continued

Example 2

Graph each inequality.

A. $n < 3$

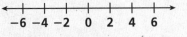

3 is not a solution, so draw an [____] circle at 3. Shade the line to the [____] of 3.

Example 3

Graph each compound inequality.

A. $m \leq -2$ or $m > 1$

First graph each [____] separately.

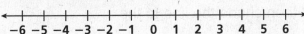

Then combine the graphs.

The solutions of $m \leq -2$ or $m > 1$ are the combined solutions of $m \leq -2$ and $m > 1$.

Check It Out!

1. Write an inequality for the situation.

There are at most 10 gallons of gas in the tank.

2. Graph the inequality.

$p \leq 2$

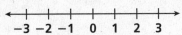

3. Graph the compound inequality.

$5 > g \geq -3$

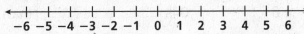

Holt McDougal Mathematics

© Houghton Mifflin Harcourt Publishing Company

Multi-Step Equations and Inequalities
Solving Inequalities by Adding or Subtracting

Lesson Objectives

Solve one-step inequalities by adding or subtracting

Additional Examples

Example 1

Solve. Then graph each solution set on a number line.

A. $n - 7 \leq 15$

$$n - 7 \leq \qquad 15$$

$\underline{+\boxed{} \qquad +\boxed{}}$ Add $\boxed{}$ to both sides.

$n \qquad \leq \quad \boxed{}$

$$\longleftarrow \!\!+\!\!\!-\!\!+\!\!\!-\!\!+\!\!\!-\!\!+\!\!\!-\!\!+\!\!\!-\!\!+\!\!\!-\!\!\longrightarrow$$
$-14 \quad -7 \quad 0 \quad 7 \quad 14 \quad 21 \quad 28 \quad 35$

Draw a $\boxed{}$ circle at 22 then shade the line to the $\boxed{}$ of 22.

Example 2

Solve. Check each answer.

A. $d + 11 > 6$

$\underline{-\boxed{} \qquad -\boxed{}}$ Subtract $\boxed{}$ from both sides.

$d \qquad > \quad \boxed{}$

Check

$$d + 11 > 6$$

$\boxed{} + 11 \overset{?}{>} 6$ 0 is $\boxed{}$ than -5. Substitute 0 for d.

$11 \overset{?}{>} 6 \checkmark$

194   **Holt McDougal Mathematics**

© Houghton Mifflin Harcourt Publishing Company

Multi-Step Equations and Inequalities

Solving Inequalities by Adding or Subtracting, continued

Example 3

Edgar's August profit of $137 was at least $20 higher than his July profit. What was July's profit?

August profit	was at least	$20 higher than	July's profit
$ ☐	≥	☐	+ p

$$137 \geq 20 + p$$

$- \boxed{} \quad - \boxed{}$ Subtract $\boxed{}$ from both sides.

$\boxed{} \geq p$ Rewrite the inequality.

$p \leq \boxed{}$

Edgar's profit in July was at most $ ☐ .

Check It Out!

1. Solve. Then graph the solution set on a number line.

$$b - 14 \geq -8$$

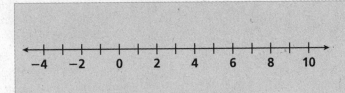

2. Solve. Check the answer.

$$a + 15 \leq 20$$

3. Last year, the football team had at least 8 more takeaways than last year. Last year they had 10 takeaways. How many takeaways did they have this year?

Holt McDougal Mathematics

Multi-Step Equations and Inequalities

Solving Inequalities by Multiplying or Dividing

Lesson Objectives

Solve one-step inequalities by multiplying or dividing

Additional Examples

Example 1

Solve.

A. $\dfrac{c}{4} \le -4$

$$\dfrac{c}{4} \le -4$$

$(\boxed{})\,\dfrac{c}{4} \le (\boxed{})(-4)$ 　　Multiply both sides by $\boxed{}$.

$$c \le \boxed{}$$

Example 2

Solve. Check each answer.

A.　　$5a \ge 23$

$\boxed{} \ge \boxed{}$ 　　　Divide both sides by $\boxed{}$.

$a \ge \boxed{}$, or $\boxed{}$

Check

$5a \ge 23$

$5(\boxed{}) \overset{?}{\ge} 23$ 　　5 is $\boxed{}$ than $4\dfrac{3}{5}$. Substitute 5 for a.

$25 \overset{?}{\ge} 23$ ✓

Holt McDougal Mathematics

© Houghton Mifflin Harcourt Publishing Company

LESSON 6

Multi-Step Equations and Inequalities

Solving Inequalities by Multiplying or Dividing, continued

Example 3

It cost Josh $85 to make candles for the craft fair. How many candles must he sell at $4.00 each to make a profit?

Since profit is the amount earned _____ the amount spent, Josh

needs to earn _____ than $85.

Let c represent the number of candles that must be sold.

$4c$ ☐ 85

$\dfrac{4c}{\boxed{}}$ ☐ $\dfrac{85}{\boxed{}}$ Divide both sides by ☐.

c ☐ ☐

Josh cannot sell 0.25 candle, so he needs to sell at least ☐ candles,

or more than ☐ candles, to earn a profit.

Check It Out!

1. Solve.

$\dfrac{r}{-3} > 0.9$

2. Solve. Check your answer.

$6b \geq 25$

3. It cost the class $15 to make cookies for the bake sale. How many cookies must they sell at 10¢ each to make a profit?

197   **Holt McDougal Mathematics**

© Houghton Mifflin Harcourt Publishing Company

Multi-Step Equations and Inequalities
Solving Multi-Step Inequalities

Lesson Objectives

Solve simple multi-step inequalities

Additional Examples

Example 1

Solve. Then graph each solution set on a number line.

A. $\dfrac{y}{2} - 6 > 1$

$\underline{+\boxed{}\quad +\boxed{}}$ Add $\boxed{}$ to both sides.

$\dfrac{y}{2} > \boxed{}$

$(\boxed{})\dfrac{y}{2} > (\boxed{})7$ Multiply both sides by $\boxed{}$.

$y > \rule{2cm}{0.5cm}$

$\longleftarrow \!\!\! \begin{array}{ccccccc} | & | & | & | & | & | & | \\ -21 & -14 & -7 & 0 & 7 & 14 & 21 \end{array} \!\!\! \longrightarrow$

Example 2

Solve. Then graph each solution set on a number line.

A. $6y - 5 - 2y < 11$

$\boxed{}y - 5 < 11$ Combine like terms.

$\underline{+\boxed{}\quad +\boxed{}}$ Add $\boxed{}$ to both sides.

$4y < \boxed{}$

$\dfrac{4y}{4} < \dfrac{16}{4}$ Divide both sides by 4.

$y < \rule{3cm}{0.5cm}$

Holt McDougal Mathematics

© Houghton Mifflin Harcourt Publishing Company

Multi-Step Equations and Inequalities

LESSON 7

Solving Multi-Step Inequalities, continued

Example 3

Sun-Li has $30 to spend at the carnival. Admission is $5, and each ride costs $2. What is the greatest number of rides she can ride?

Let r represent the number of rides Sun-Li can ride.

$5 + 2r \leq 30$

$-\boxed{}\ -\boxed{}$ Subtract $\boxed{}$ from both sides.

$2r \leq \boxed{}$

$\boxed{} \leq \boxed{}$ Divide both sides by $\boxed{}$.

$r \leq \boxed{}$, or $\boxed{}$

Sun-Li can ride only a whole number of rides, so the most she can ride

is $\boxed{}$.

Check It Out!

1. Solve. Then graph each solution set on a number line.

$-9x + 4 \leq 31$

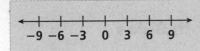

2. Solve. Then graph the solution set on a number line.

$6 + 5(2 - x) \leq 41$

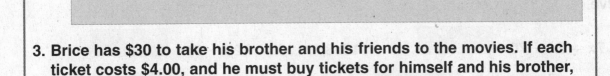

3. Brice has $30 to take his brother and his friends to the movies. If each ticket costs $4.00, and he must buy tickets for himself and his brother, what is the greatest number of friends he can invite?

Holt McDougal Mathematics

LESSON 11 | Multi-Step Equations and Inequalities
Chapter Review

1 Solving Two-Step Equations

Solve. Check each answer.

1. $3x + 9 = 72$

2. $2q - 7 = 13$

3. $-4y + 11 = 75$

4. $38 = 7p - 18$

5. $\frac{z}{5} + 1 = 8$

6. $\frac{x}{-3} - 9 = 10$

7. A salesperson earned a paycheck for $2,750. The paycheck was a $500 bonus plus a flat rate for three seminars attended. What was the salesperson's rate of pay for each seminar?

2 Solving Multi-Step Equations

Solve.

8. $2y + 8 + 4y = 44$

9. $11c - 12 - 2c = 6$

10. $14 = -2x + 14 + x$

11. $3z + 4 - 6z = -20$

12. $3(x + 7) + 5 = 65$

13. $12 + 2(p - 5) = -6$

3 Solving Equations with Variables on Both Sides

Group the terms with variables on one side of the equal sign, and simplify.

14. $6x = 2x + 24$

15. $-4y + 10 = 6y$

16. $3c - 32 = -5c$

Solve.

17. $7x = 2x + 70$

18. $3p + 14 = -2p + 74$

19. $\frac{2}{5}x + 19 = \frac{1}{5}x + 21$

20. $-4 - y = 7y - 36$

© Houghton Mifflin Harcourt Publishing Company

Holt McDougal Mathematics

Multi-Step Equations and Inequalities

Chapter Review, continued

4 Inequalities

Write an inequality for each situation.

21. There are no more than 25 students in each class.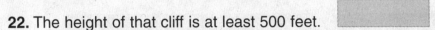

22. The height of that cliff is at least 500 feet.

Graph each compound inequality.

23. $x > 1$ or $x \le -2$ 24. $-2 \le x < 3$ 25. $4 < y \le 7$

5 Solving Inequalities by Adding or Subtracting

Solve. Then graph each solution set on a number line.

26. $x + 1 < 10$ 27. $y - 3 \ge -2$ 28. $-12 < p - 8$

6 Solving Inequalities by Multiplying or Dividing

Solve.

29. $\dfrac{x}{6} < 2$ 30. $\dfrac{y}{-2} \ge 1$ 31. $-5y \ge 15$

32. JoAnne needs to raise $150. How many complete hours must she baby-sit at a rate of $4.50 per hour, in order to have enough money?

7 Solving Multi-Step Inequalities

Solve. Then graph each solution set on a number line.

33. $3x + 3 \le 30$ 34. $\dfrac{y}{5} + 7 > 19$ 35. $-15 \ge 5z + 6 - 2z$

Holt McDougal Mathematics

© Houghton Mifflin Harcourt Publishing Company

Multi-Step Equations and Inequalities
Big Ideas

Answer these questions to summarize the important concepts from Chapter 11 in your own words.

1. Explain how to solve the equation $8x - 7 = 57$.

2. Explain how to solve the equation $4y + 9 - y = -3$.

3. Explain how to solve the equation $5z + 6 = -2z + 27$.

4. Explain how to solve the inequality $-8a \geq 32$.

5. Explain when to draw a closed circle or an open circle when graphing inequalities.

For more review of Chapter 11:

- Complete the Chapter 11 Study Guide and Review in your textbook.
- Complete the Ready to Go On quizzes in your textbook.

© Houghton Mifflin Harcourt Publishing Company

Holt McDougal Mathematics